Praise for *The First Step*

"Take up this book and a very modern master of spirituality takes your hand and leads you inward, closer to God."

—Rabbi Irving Greenberg
National Jewish Resource Center

"An experiential, living, Jewish spirituality that is resonant with the New Age."

—Eugene Gendlin, Ph.D.
University of Chicago
Author of *Focusing*

"What he has to say about work, marriage, divorce, the pace of life in our modern world, and how to cope with a myriad of problems we human beings face addresses all of human-kind."

—Joshu Sasaki Roshi

"The profound is made simple and the simple is disclosed to be profound. This 'Guide for the New Jewish Spirit' can further the awakening of non-Jews as well."

—Robert Masters, Ph.D.
The Foundation for Mind Research

"Rabbi Zalman Schachter-Shalomi is infusing Judaism with a new spirit .... He is the spearhead of the new movement in Judaism to sound the call for spiritual awakening."

—Pir Vilayat Inayat Khan

". . . a *Duties of the Heart* for today's cosmopolitan . . ."

—David Tulin, Educator

". . . a beautiful handbook to help the reader attune to the Inner Spirit."

—Sri Swami Satchidananda
Founder-Director:
Integral Yoga Institutes

By Zalman Schachter-Shalomi
FRAGMENTS OF A FUTURE SCROLL
THE ENCOUNTER: (YEHIDUT), A STUDY OF COUNSELLING
IN HASIDISM

By Donald Gropman
SAY IT AIN'T SO, JOE!

THE FIRST STEP
A GUIDE FOR THE
NEW JEWISH SPIRIT

by Reb Zalman Schachter-Shalomi
with Donald Gropman

 BANTAM BOOKS
TORONTO · NEW YORK · LONDON · SYDNEY

THE FIRST STEP: A GUIDE FOR THE NEW JEWISH SPIRIT
A Bantam Book / February 1983

PRINTING HISTORY
Quotation from Four Hasidic Masters translated by
Elie Wiesel (University of Notre Dame Press, Notre Dame, 1978).
Used by permission.

Book designed by Renée Gelman.

Library of Congress Catalog Card No. 82-90328

ISBN 0-553-01418-8

Published simultaneously in the United States and Canada

Bantam Books are published by Bantam Books, Inc. Its trademark, consisting of the words "Bantam Books" and the por-
trayal of a rooster, is Registered in U.S. Patent and Trademark
Office and in other countries. Marca Registrada. Bantam
Books, Inc., 666 Fifth Avenue, New York, New York 10103.

PRINTED IN THE UNITED STATES OF AMERICA

0 9 8 7 6 5 4 3 2 1

MUCH I LEARNED
FROM MY TEACHERS

The rebbes of Lubavitch, Bobov, Bratzlav, Izhbitza,
Piasetzno and Bergscaz

MORE FROM MY FRIENDS
Reb Gedalyah Kenig and Rev. Howard Thurman,
whose memory is a blessing

BUT MOST OF ALL FROM MY STUDENTS
(Ta'anit 7:a)
Whose search to be intimate with God stimulated
this book.

—Z. S-S

For Gabrielle, Sonya and Adam.

—D.G.

THE WAY OF
TEACHING

The holy Baal Shem Tov once came upon one of his colleagues teaching the secret wisdom of Jewish mysticism (*Kabbalah*) in public. Later, in private, he chided his colleague for his way of teaching, saying: "You are teaching the literal words of the secrets to the people."

His colleague responded, "And you, Rebbe, don't you also teach the secret wisdom of the *Kabbalah* to the masses?"

The Baal Shem Tov replied, "Yes, we both draw from the same source. But you teach it as it is written on the page of a book and I teach it as it applies to people in real life."

Rabbi Israel ben Eliezer, the Baal Shem Tov (Master of the Good Name), founded Hasidism in the eighteenth century.

CONTENTS

A NOTE TO
THE READER

If you happened to pick up this book by chance, good. Perhaps it will be a stroke of luck that may lead to beneficial changes in your life. But more likely than not, your encounter with this book is not an accident. It is another step in a journey of spiritual growth and change you've already begun, a journey you hope will lead you to a more meaningful and nourishing Jewish way of life.

I imagine you, the reader, as a seeker in search of at least two things. One is a *way* to express the spiritual stirrings you have felt in yourself, and another is a *practical method* with which you can develop that holy source within you so that it will begin to flow freely.

You are not alone in this journey. Jews everywhere are on a similar quest. In large part, this quest is motivated by a malaise, a feeling that there *must* be more in Judaism than the cut–and–dried version frequently encountered in contemporary services.

All too often, people feel left out. Services tend to be conducted in a formalistic way, and many worshippers don't participate actively and don't know what's going on. A major problem is the lack of *feeling* or *affect*—there is no laughter, there are no tears, nor are these natural human expressions encouraged, as if God would be embarrassed by such displays in His house of worship.

We need new models, alternative ways of practicing Judaism, but until recently few have been generally available. It is the aim of this book to begin to fill that need. This book does not pretend to be the last word on the matter. On the contrary, it is our hope that it will encourage others to share their thoughts, experiences, and know-how about getting more out of being a Jew.

The overall process we will pursue is aimed at increasing and enriching our relationship with God. God has many roles in our lives: He is Father, She is Mother, the Lord is an all-encompassing Being for Which we don't even have a good word-name.

God is internalized in our souls and consciousness; God is projected externally onto the cosmos. God is immanent; God is manifest. But what God is like is up to each soul to decide. We each create our image of God from the feelings of our hearts, the insights of our dreams, from our memories and our reflections, from our interactions with the universe and each other. In forming this image, external philosophies are of no help. Everybody has to do this task for him- or herself. So when the word God appears in this book, you needn't assume anything else except this functional orientation.

TRADITION IS ORGANIC

In moments of grace, I'm aware that God is available to me, in consciousness, love, and energy. He's there for all of us; all we have to do is find Him and take hold. The problem is that many of us are confused and disappointed. We have tried, but we haven't gotten far enough.

We wander in one direction for a while, then another. But it is disheartening: the maps are old and the roads have changed. In addressing this problem, we have tried to sketch a contemporary road map for living in the Jewish universe and to provide a practical guide for using that map.

The coordinates for our map are derived from the tradition of Jewish mysticism. The principles which inform this tradition are: 1) that an act be appropriate to the place, time, and people present, and 2) that it be in organic harmony with life. In this way, one who lives the tradition increases awareness and grows spiritually. This tradition has power. Like everything else in the universe, it is evolving and, in some measure, it is available to you now.

As you will soon see, we are not as interested in theory as in *practice*. We are interested in *what works*. Thirty-five years of my own wrestling with the eternal Jewish questions have not left me with a static set of rules and dogmas. What I've found instead is a set of actions and rituals which have been tested empirically by my own observations and experiences. These rituals have proven useful and practical for being a *mensch* (ideal, caring human being).

With your hard work, honest intentions, and God's blessings, this book can point you in the right direction and start you on your journey to regain the life-giving treasures that are your birthright as a human being and as a Jew.

FRIEND
TO FRIEND

Let me tell you something about my background so that you'll have an idea of the context from which I speak.

I was born in Poland in 1924 and grew up in Vienna, where my family moved when I was young. My father was a Hasid who developed a great interest in Western ways and ideas. He remained a devout Jew (he taught me to pray), but he also steered my education toward a pluralistic path—I went to *yeshiva* and at the same time attended a leftist Zionist high school where I learned Latin and modern Hebrew. I danced the *hora* with Marxist Zionists and also celebrated the farewell to the Sabbath with Orthodox anti-Zionists.

Like all the other Jews of Europe, our lives were disrupted by Hitler, though it was our fortune to survive. To keep ahead of the Nazi hordes, we left Vienna and moved to Antwerp. In those days I was one of the many Jews who felt angry, dispossessed, and full of poison. One day I found myself in an Orthodox study house in Antwerp, challenging the teacher to answer the many questions and doubts I shared with everyone growing up in the chaos of those times. The teacher, a very understanding and well-educated man, let me get rid of all my poison without cutting me off. He then showed me that not only were my questions not stupid, but that they were, in fact, legitimate ones raised by others before me. He suggested that if I could feel confidence in the way in which they raised those questions, perhaps I ought to feel confidence too in the way they answered them.

This approach led me into a world which was very, very exciting. It turned out that my teacher was a Lubavitcher Hasid. Because of him, I ended up coming to America and attending a Lubavitcher *yeshiva*. My chance encounter with the Hasid in Antwerp was my introduction to Jewish mysticism.

WHAT I FOUND IN HASIDISM

Hasidism, founded in the eighteenth century, is a branch of the Jewish mystical tradition. Since then it has flourished in several schools of thought, one of which is Chabad Hasidism, whose emphasis is intellectual and contemplative. I was drawn to the Lubavitch tradition, a form of Chabad, because of its promise that one could become adept enough to attain certain mystical experiences in this lifetime. The various tales told by the Hasidim about their Rebbes concern the attainment of such experiences. I also liked the nature of the relationship between the Rebbe and the individual Hasid. In this kind of Hasidism, the Rebbe shows you the way, but you have to do the work yourself—rather than hang onto his coattails.

My flight from the Nazis did not end in Belgium. Before it was over I spent some time in an internment camp in Vichy, France. From there I crossed the Mediterranean Sea to North Africa. A banana boat took me to West Africa. Then I went by freighter to the West Indies and, finally, on to New York.

I enrolled in the Lubavitcher yeshiva in Brooklyn and spent the next ten years of my life studying and preparing to be a rabbi. This training was intense and served to ground me in the basic tenets of Jewish mysticism, which are grouped under the catch-all term kabbalah (literally, "that which is received").

Mystics claim that you can experience the Infinite right now, that beneath the surface of the obvious exists the Divine. Here, of course, we are in the domain of the soul. To talk of the soul is to admit that a human being has needs that cannot be met in the physical world alone—the world of things. The fact is that no matter how much money you spend on your wardrobe, your spirit might still be in rags, and even the most conspicuous, expensive sports car can't drive you to the place in which you feel good about yourself or your relationship with God.

WHAT I FOUND IN THE CHAPEL

After ten years of intensive training and education, I was ordained as a rabbi. The late, sainted Lubavitcher Rebbe then sent me to New England, where I taught at yeshivas he'd helped to found and served as rabbi to several congregations. It was during this time—the early and mid-1950s—that I began to feel the need for more education and a wider range of experience, but I wasn't sure what I was looking for.

Up to this point in my life, my religious education had taken place entirely within the Jewish world. Then I enrolled in graduate school at Boston University, where I earned a master's degree in the psychology of religion, and where, more importantly, I had the good fortune to meet Howard Thurman, then Dean of the Chapel at the university.

When I attended Boston University, I lived in New Bedford, Massachusetts, a two-hour drive away. In the winter, I had to be on my way while it was still dark outside and too early to say the morning prayers, so I'd leave at five o'clock in order to arrive at seven and have an hour for prayer and a bit of breakfast before my first class at eight.

The problem was to find a suitable place to pray. The only building open at that early hour was the chapel, but this too presented a dilemma. In the main chapel upstairs were statues of Jesus and the Evangelists, and I didn't feel comfortable praying there. Downstairs was a smaller chapel for meditation, but I was inhibited by a big brass cross on the altar table. Finally I chose a public room in the chapel building, found myself a corner facing the east, toward Jerusalem, and used that as my morning prayer place.

One morning, when I'd just completed my prayers, a middle-aged black man came into the room and said in a casual way, "I've seen you here several times. Wouldn't you like to say your prayers in the small chapel?"

I shrugged my shoulders, not knowing what to say. The man was so unpretentious that I thought he might have been the person who took care of the building. His offer was so forthcoming that I didn't want to hurt his feelings—how could I explain that I couldn't pray in the chapel because of the cross on the altar?

He looked at me and said, "Why don't you stop by the chapel tomorrow morning and see? Maybe you'd be comfortable saying your prayers there."

The next morning, out of curiosity, I looked into the chapel. Two candles were burning in brass candlesticks and the big brass cross was gone. The ornate large Bible was open to the Book of Psalms. From then on I said my morning prayers in the chapel.

Some time later I read an announcement about a new course in spiritual disciplines and resources which would include labs for spiritual exercises, to be taught by the Dean of the Chapel. The course intrigued me, but I was apprehensive about taking it. The Dean of the Chapel was also a minister and I worried that he might feel obliged to try to convert me. After some thought, I made an appointment to speak with him about my concerns.

When I walked into the office, the friendly black man from the chapel was sitting behind the desk, none other than Dean Thurman himself. He smiled and offered me a mug of coffee. I felt a little ashamed of my initial assumption; I should have understood from our first encounter that this was a man to be trusted, but I was still hesitant.

"Dean Thurman," I said, "I would like to take your course, but I don't know if my anchor chains are long enough."

He put his coffee mug on his desk and began to look at his hands. He turned them palms up, then palms down. The back of his hands was very dark and his palms were very light. He turned them back and forth, looking at them, as if considering the light and dark sides of an argument. This lasted for several minutes, but it felt like hours to me. He did what he was doing with such a calm certainty that he seemed to possess great power. Suddenly he spoke. "Don't you trust the *Ruach Hakodesh*?"

I was stunned. He'd used the Hebrew words for the Spirit of Holiness, something I had not expected from a gentile. And in so doing, he brought that great question home to me in a particularly strong way. I began to tremble and walked out of his office without answering him.

For the next three weeks I went through torment struggling with the question. Did I indeed trust the *Ruach Hakodesh*, trust It enough to have faith in my self-identity as a Jew? Or was I holding back, fearful of testing my belief in an encounter with another religion, unnerved by the prospect of trusting my soul to a non-Jew? If I was fearful, it meant I did not truly believe.

Finally, I realized that his question could have only one answer. "Don't you trust the *Ruach Hakodesh*?" Dean Thurman had said. I had to say, "Yes, I do," and I signed up for his course.

The course was marvelous, and I learned a great deal, especially from his use of labs. In the labs we experimented with various spiritual exercises. These frequently took the form of guided meditations. In one kind of exercise, we were instructed to translate an experience from one sense to another—we would read a psalm several times, then listen to a piece by Bach, to "hear" the meaning of the psalm in the sounds of the music. Another exercise was to "see" music as an abstract design moving through space. In these ways, our senses were released from their usual narrow constraints and freed to tune into the cosmos, to touch God.

People seldom have those primary experiences in religion referred to by William James, Aldous Huxley, and others. Without this first-hand knowledge, the study of religion is impoverished. Such labs allow the student to understand what is being taught. Providing these primary experiences is now part of my method. They turn out to be very, very important in the spiritual growth of the individual.

In the exchanges with Dean Thurman and the other members of the class, I learned an important lesson which is still at the center of my thinking: Judaism and all the other western religions are suffering from having become 4ererbalized and underexperienced.

Someone else's description of ecstasy or spiritual at-one-ness, given second- or third-hand, is not enough. I wanted to have the experience myself, and I'd like to help make it possible for other people to have it too. That is part of what a living, breathing religion is about.

THE SHAMAN BLOWS THE SHOFAR

The Hasidic approach to the religious experience aims at empirical realization. I use empirical in its classic meaning—basing my knowledge of the religious experience on direct observation and experiment. As an empiricist, I recognize the validity of non-Jewish religious experience, so over the years I've explored other religions, as well as other methods for enhancing spiritual growth. These forays have provided me with validation for my own religion.

A few years ago, in Calgary, Canada, I participated in a symposium on mysticism, with spokesmen for several other traditions. Among us was a medicine man from the Blood Indian Reservation, Brother Rufus Goodstriker. We were all put up at a modern plastic motel, a place which didn't seem to hold much promise for a group of mystics. But the setting was glorious—to the east, the Canadian prairie stretched for miles; and to the west, the Canadian Rockies soared into the sky.

When I woke up the first morning and began preparing to say my prayers, I remembered where I was and decided to go up to the roof. So I took my *talis* (prayer shawl), *tefilin* (phylacteries—small black boxes, containing prayer parchments that are worn on the left arm and forehead during morning prayers), and a *shofar* (hollowed ram's horn) and rode the elevator up to the top floor. I found the door to the roof and pushed against it slowly in case it made a lot of noise or touched off an alarm. But it made just a slight noise; I closed it softly behind me.

The sky was still dark in the west, but in the east there were streaks of light. The roof was a forest of air conditioners, vent pipes, and chimneys, but I found myself a corner facing the east and began to get into my prayers.

After a few minutes, I heard the door open again and Brother Rufus stepped out onto the roof. He, too, had a small bundle under his arm. We acknowledged each other's presence with wordless nods. He also took up a position facing east and began to perform *his* morning ritual.

First he took out a prayer blanket, which reminded me of my *talis*. Then he lit a small charcoal fire, offered some incense, and made a burnt offering of a pinch of meal or flour. Facing the east with his arms raised in the air, he swayed back and forth, chanting in a language I did not understand. But I did not have to understand the language to know that he was calling to God. At the moment of sunrise, he placed a small whistle to his lips and blew a sharp note in every direction.

I continued my own prayers and concluded by blowing my *shofar*. Then I wrapped up my things and saw that Brother Rufus was doing the same. He approached me and asked in a gentle, direct way, "May I please see your instruments? If I were at home I would have had a sweat lodge this morning to be ritually clean before I touch them. Here at this place all I could have was a shower. Is that all right?"

I told him it was and unwrapped my things. He looked at the *tefilin*. "Ah, rawhide," he said. Then he handled them and noticed they were sewn together with natural gut, not with machine-made thread. He nodded to let me know he understood the significance of using gut, a natural material with an animal's power, instead of cotton or nylon.

Then he carefully examined the knots in the *tefilin*, ran his fingertips over them, and said with respect, "Noble knots." Next he shook the *tefilin* and heard something move. "What is inside the black box?" he asked. I told him there was a piece of parchment on which was written God's name and other holy words. He nodded and I saw respect on his face. I knew that he understood my prayer instruments and my prayers.

Then he looked at my brightly striped *talis* and thought it was beautiful—he loved the colors, which bore some resemblance to the colors of his own prayer blanket. He examined the *tzitzis* (the knotted fringes at the corners of the *talis*) and saw the five double knots and the windings of blue thread that create a very specific design. "What's the message?" he asked, revealing to me that he also understood that such designs are not random, but deliberate.

After a few moments, he picked up the *shofar* and looked it over. "Ram's horn," he commented. "We use a whistle made from an eagle bone. May I blow it?"

He blew a few loud notes through the ram's horn, handed it back, and simply said, "Of course, it's much better than cow."

For a moment I thought, "Better for what?" But Brother Rufus was a medicine man. He knew that you blow animal bones to blow the demons away, to clear the air, to connect with God, to bring about change, to say to the sleeping soul, "Hey, there, wake up! Pay attention!"

At every step of his examination of my sacred prayer tools, Brother Rufus asked the right questions. He was in tune with the technology of religious artifacts and he understood them. He, coming from a very different world, approached my religious instruments as if they were not so different from his own, and he affirmed each one.

His response reminded me of the common element of all religion, the inner experience which transcends external variations and differences. As Reb Nachman of Bratzlav said, "The Holy Spirit shouts forth from the tales of the gentiles, too."

I do not believe that anyone has the exclusive franchise on the Truth. What we have is a good approximation, for Jews, of how to get there. Ultimately, each person creates a way that fits his own situation. While there are differences between Jewish and non-Jewish approaches to mysticism in specific methods, observances, and rituals, there are no differences in the impact of the experiences themselves. When it comes to what I call the "heart stuff," all approaches overlap.

ADULT TO ADULT

This is why I approach you as a friend, to speak to you about some things that have worked for me and for a number of other people in our quest to do a better job with our lives. The process I'm talking about is the conscious experience of waking up—as human beings and as Jews.

But why as a friend? Why don't I speak to you as a rabbi? The answer has to do with my intention and my attitude. If I were to speak to you only out of my role as rabbi, it would imply that you had come to me in a very specific way and said, "I have accepted the basic tenets of Judaism and I've committed my life to them. Now I, as a rabbi, ask you to give me the guidance of the tradition." But I want to speak to everyone, to Jews and non-Jews, to Jews who have accepted Judaism, and to Jews who are uncertain.

And my attitude is different. I am not primarily interested in elucidating the Law and telling you what to do. I
do not believe there is much energy in the authoritarian
mode, and when I speak solely as rabbi, it is difficult to
avoid some of the trappings of authoritarianism. But I do
believe there is energy to be generated and shared in the
give-and-take between equals.

THERE'S ONLY ONE WAY
FOR US TO GET IT TOGETHER—
TOGETHER

No matter how well you think you've put *yourself* together, the rest of us (the world) can intrude pretty easily
and unravel you. Imagine that you've left your apartment
in the morning, feeling calm and focused. Now imagine
yourself getting onto whatever public transportation you
take to get to work, or relive driving through the morning
rush hour traffic. Either way, how do you feel when you
get there? Probably frazzled.

Of course, if you lead a vacuum-packed contemplative
life in the relative serenity of the countryside, your solo
practices can have a greater and more enduring effect on
your everyday life. But most of us live in the cities where
our lives are pressure-packed and the pressures seem to
be increasing all the time. In the city, we have a greater
and more immediate effect on each other: density breeds
more frequent contact. In the city, it is not only important
that we take care of ourselves (perhaps by meditating or
performing some other spiritual exercise which focuses
our being, and puts us more in touch with the universe),
but it is equally important that everyone else in the city
does something along the same lines.

The point is this: when we are doing spiritual work,

sooner or later we need other people—community. We need others with whom we can share our efforts, who can provide a matrix for our experiences and generate an energy field.

We need people with whom, for example, we can share our tears and joy. I mean this literally. Crying publicly in a group that honors and respects our tears is a very rich experience, entirely different from crying in private. So the task is to find a suitable group, one that can provide enough intimate support to nourish each member's spiritual work.

For Jews who are interested in finding such a support group, the first words that probably come to mind are congregation or synagogue. It is a natural association, but there is a problem. Today most American Jewish congregations do not promote intimacy.

It is difficult, if not impossible, to generate a sense of group intimacy in a large congregation of people who sit in their pews staring straight ahead, not daring to be in touch with their neighbors. To understand how we arrived at such a state, we must look at our early history in this country.

FROM CONGREGATION TO HAVURA

In Europe, where most American Jews come from, each city or town had one kehila, a central Jewish congregation which maintained separate synagogues for different groups. In charge of the central or great synagogue was a Rov, the Head Rabbi, who was presiding magistrate in both meanings—teacher and judge. Frequently, the branch synagogues were organized around guilds or trades (like woodchoppers or bakers), whose members provided encouragement and other support for each other.

This model prevailed for many years in Europe, but it was not easily adaptable to the very different conditions in the United States.

For one thing, the newly developing American Jewish communities were usually composed of Jews from different geographical and linguistic backgrounds. This alone would have made it difficult for the centralized model to continue, but there was an additional element, the American concept of religious freedom. This most basic American value meant at least two things to Jews. First, they felt free to reject or openly practice their religion; and second, they felt free to practice it in their own ways. Translated into direct action, this meant that when a few Jews did not like the practices or atmosphere in this or that *shul*, they felt free to start their own.

At first, Jews banded together on the basis of *landsmanschaft*, which is to say, a common origin in the Old World (usually a specific city, town, or *shtetl*). These *landsmanschaft* groupings were appropriate as long as people lived near each other, in one of the boroughs of New York, or in the Jewish neighborhoods of other large cities.

But when Jews became geographically mobile and dispersed from the older Jewish communities, other lines of organization emerged. One was a shared preference for a particular rite: the Eastern European rite; the Sephardic rite; the Ashkenazic rite. And around these preferences, Jews once again organized themselves into congregations.

As time passed, these congregations established facilities to take care of the purely ceremonial needs that Jews have in their rites of passage: births, namings, Hebrew teaching, Bar and (more recently) Bas Mitzvah, marriage, and death.

In the 1920s and 1930s, the total Jewish community polarized into Orthodox, Conservative, and Reform congregations, with Reconstructionism emerging in the 1930s. Within each of these denominational groups, the European model of organization was repeated on a smaller scale. In its day, it proved to be an efficient model. The problem was that it continued to exist after it had outlived its usefulness. Eventually, it gave rise to those jumbo-jet congregations in which you had one rabbi-pilot and one cantor copilot and everybody else strapped into their seatbelts and told, "If you don't move very much, and if you don't walk around, and if you let the stewards and stewardesses serve you very quickly, we'll have you at your landing spot, which is out of here and down to the social hour in a very short time."

But that system is not very conducive to the kinds of experience human beings need in order to be fully awakened, fully alive. More and more, the real experience, the genuine content, was pushed out of the synagogue. Rites of passage got streamlined and standard-packed. For example, you could have your individual wedding ceremony, provided it was read from the standard ritual. Your names inserted in the blank spaces would be the only personal note. Such congregational practices could not fulfill spiritual needs.

We know that there are other ways to perform a wedding ceremony. As a friend, I sit with a couple and ask what experiences would help them infuse their lives with meaning, sanctity, and commitment so that they will be able to stand each other and work through all the extremes that two people undergo and yet still find the stability and the vocation of their relationship. When you put the task this way, you do not talk about florists, caterers, and what clothes to wear, or recite the stipulations of an impersonal legal document. You begin to talk from an entirely different perspective.

FROM JUMBO JET TO THE LIVING ROOM

By the 1960s, more and more young Jews had become involved in personal growth experiences, particularly those rooted in the Orient. It was a period of great experimentation—group living, mind-altering drugs, humanistic psychologies, changing sexual attitudes and mores, environmentalism, feminism, organic consciousness, meditation, biofeedback, and others.

Many Jews who had participated in some of these experiences, and wanted to approach and practice Judaism in light of their new awareness, felt there was no place for them to turn. In 1968, a group of us—from different backgrounds and with varying levels of Jewish education—gathered in the Boston area at the invitation of Rabbi-Dr. Arthur Green; we formed what became Havurat Shalom, the first of the Havurot, which by now has grown into the national Havura movement. Our concern was to create a group which could function democratically as a "family of friends," who shared the goal of spiritual growth. We wanted to focus on the religious experience itself, and were not bound by any preconceived notion of what a religious service ought to be, or at least not as it had been formulated in most existing congregations.

We were trying to create a meaningful alternative to the jumbo-jet congregations. A nonhierarchical, democratic model was, therefore, very important to us—nobody would be passively strapped into his or her seat. Everyone would contribute and have a turn to be pilot. Women would participate fully; it was obvious to all of us that women were equal members and leaders. We were seeking spiritual democracy, and our goal was to create a group in which we could realize our vision of what practicing being Jews *could be*. Our vision was exciting and our aims were high, though the details were in the process of evolving. We imagined a setting in which the inner experience of our souls' search for God could take place with group support.

It was a thrilling way to approach spiritual work—the potential seemed limitless. It was also a point of view which released a great deal of energy. This book is written from that point of view, and it is addressed to those who wish to see life from that point of view.

Rx FOR A
WORKING JEW

We do strange things to time. We invent games in which we stop and start time at our pleasure: Time in! Time out! When some of us go to work, we punch a time clock. Between "important" events, we kill time. When somebody breaks the law, we punish him by making him serve time. Television gives us the Six O'Clock News, the Eleven O'Clock News, the Today Show, the Tonight Show, the Tomorrow Show. And TV also gives us prime time. This is how we measure and evaluate time now. We have bought a concept of time as a standardized commodity, and the price we pay is consciousness. What we lose in the exchange is organic time. And the more we lose touch with organic time, the more automated we become.

Commodity time is good for industries, banking, business, and television, but it's not good for living life. In order to survive the regimen of nine-to-five time, we need the counter regimen of organic time, which changes texture with the turning of our planet. Corporate convenience cannot set the clock by which life is lived. Life is lived in organic time; it runs on the ebb and tide of forces which exist in the universe.

17

Time as commodity is out of phase with time as it flows in nature. The Jewish notion is to bring these two aspects of time into sync with each other. Judaism says: Sunrise . . . sunset. Six days and the Sabbath. New moon, full moon. Equinox and solstice. The full moon of the vernal equinox is Passover. The full moon of the autumnal equinox is Succot (the Feast of the Tabernacles). The last phase of the moon in the last phase of the sun is Chanukah.

These holidays come at their organic time, coinciding with the realities in nature. Looking from a larger perspective within the Jewish calendar, we can see patterns of one year, a seven-year cycle, ending in a sabbatical year, and then seven seven-year cycles, ending in a Jubilee Year. "Six years shall you sow your field, and six years you shall prune your vineyard and gather in its fruit. But the seventh year shall be a sabbath of solemn rest for the land, a sabbath for the Lord: you shall neither sow your field nor prune your vineyard. . . . And you shall count seven sabbaths of years, seven times seven years. . . . And you shall hallow the fiftieth year and proclaim liberty throughout all the land to all its inhabitants: it shall be a jubilee for you; and you shall return every man to his possession, and you shall return every man to his family" (Leviticus 25). As a result of these patterns, we are constantly involved in an incredible rhythm of rhythms, the pulsing life of the universe.

The rhythm of organic time is inherent in all life. It is not something that is only outside of us; it is within us on all levels of our beings. Inside us there is also an ebb and tide during day and night. And there are the rhythms of digestion that go on all the time; and the faster rhythms of pulse and heartbeat; and the still faster rhythms of exchanges that take place in the lungs; and the rapid interactions within the capillaries; and finally, there are the ultrafast rhythms that take place in the nervous system and in the brain. And on the molecular and submolecular levels, rhythms occur in angstrom wave lengths, with millions of reversals per second.

Organic time is actually humming inside us. It is one of the voices of God. Reb Nachman of Bratzlav called it "the voice of my Beloved—the pulse. If you want to know God," he said, "you need only listen to His voice within. You need never be lonely for Him or out of touch with His inner spirit; you can always touch your pulse and say, 'Oh, there You are.'"

We all understand that the better we play the game with commodity time, the more money we make. But the better we dance with organic time, the better we live. The purpose of earning money in commodity time is to gain "control" over the world. The problem is, if we *always* play the commodity-time game, we lose touch with the sanity of organic time. To prevent this, we have the Sabbath, a time to *not do* the things we do for commodity time.

Like most people, I too play the commodity-time game, but only for six days of the week. On the seventh day, the Sabbath, I stop the game and return to organic time. The dividing line between the two kinds of time is drawn by the sunset on Friday—our acknowledgment of it is in lighting Sabbath candles. Once a week I'm placed in a full day of sane time, so that I don't lose my contact with the real universe.

The Sabbath provides a weekly dose of sane time, but in the contemporary world most of us need more than that. If we are to survive the commodity-time demands of the nine-to-five (or eight-to-six) work day, we need a *daily* dose of Sabbath or its equivalent. If this sounds unrealistic or impossible, it is because we have bought the fiction that the nature of time is established *only* by external, objective forces. We've lost sight of our own control over certain aspects of time.

From the inner, subjective point of view, time is our most malleable commodity. It is infinitely compressible and expandable. We have all had experiences that lasted only a second or two when measured by a clock, but were more eventful and "longer" than others that objectively could be measured in days or weeks. In an impending auto accident, between the moment when you know it's going to happen and the moment it actually does, subjective time expands as if the event were taking place in slow motion.

We can use time to fit our needs if we know how—and if we remember to. Doing so falls under the heading of taking care of ourselves. But first we have to know what we *are* in order to know what we need.

THE HUMAN AS A MAMMAL

We insist that we are human beings, but how much of us is uniquely human? Perhaps five or ten percent of our totality. Ninety percent of us is mammal—we're warm-blooded like a mammal, we breathe like a mammal, we defecate like a mammal. We have hair on our bodies like mammals, and like them, we nourish our infants with milk from breasts. However, we disguise our mammal in Brooks Brothers suits or designer jeans and tend to forget about it.

But if we have a pet dog, we don't forget that it's a mammal—we feed it and walk it so that it can relieve itself and get some exercise, or its digestive system won't work right. Walking is good for the dog, so we walk it every opportunity we have.

When it comes to ourselves, however, most of us treat walking intransitively. We're willing to walk Rover or Fido, but we're reluctant to walk ourselves, mainly because we are hooked to commodity time. Walking takes time, so we take the car and get there faster. Nevertheless, our mammal has to be walked. It's the responsibility of the five or ten percent of us that is our human being to take care of the mammal—which means to feed it, clothe it, rest it, see that it mates every once in a while, and all the other things which are the natural needs and functions of the mammal part of us.

Too many people neglect their mammal because they think the care will take so much time and effort, or they tell themselves they'll do it later, at some future date when they're under less stress (from work or relationships) and have more time. This is false thinking. Taking care of your mammal does not have to take much time—five minutes of exercise before you eat breakfast is a step in the right direction. Just like your dog, your mammal has to be looked after every day.

THE HUMAN AS MENSCH

After you attend to your mammal, you're ready for the next step. There's another part of you that also needs exercise—your human being. What does your human being need? It needs to be placed in a harmonious relationship with the rest of the universe. To begin to achieve this, you have to be in step with organic time. You have to be in time, to be focused on and aware of the processes that are happening now. We'll explore the unique relationship we Jews have with time a little later. For now, let's just say that timeliness and appropriateness go hand in hand. The first thing you can do to walk your human being is to be awake for the twenty or so minutes when the darkness gives way to the light during sunrise. If you've never done this, try it. It's a unique experience and you deserve to have it. In these twenty minutes nothing needs to be *done*, but much needs to be *felt*, to be *loved*: you need to love your self; to love the universe; to love your neighbors. Not doing, only loving. Just investing some time into the awareness that you have received love from the universe and that you want to give some love back—a necessary step in exercising your human being.

HUMAN BEING AS CHILD OF GOD

Every day we need to reexperience the moment in which we realized that we are integral to the universe, that we are *part* of it—not a separate entity only passing through. The Psalms tell us this: "You are my child. Today I have begotten you." When we reexperience this great awareness, we are regenerated. We need to reconnect with it every day, if only for a moment—it reestablishes our natural place in the order of the universe. When this connection happens, we are filled again with light, acceptance, and at-one-ment. For it to happen, we have to make time.

Our ability to connect with the universe is especially strong at dawn and dusk, sunrise and sunset. Whenever you can, spend that time walking your human being, walking your soul. This is how you can strengthen your connection with organic time.

The special quality of dawn and dusk doesn't have to be taught. All of creation knows about it—the birds and beasts in the forest; the creatures of the sea, who rise and fall to different levels of the ocean; in the city, even the pigeons coo at daybreak. The classic symbol of responding to dawn is the rooster crowing. He puffs himself up, throws his head back, and sings cock-a-doodle-do! It is such an important image of how to react to organic time that we Jews have made it the first of the morning blessings in the prayer book: "Blessed are You, Adonai, Cosmic Majesty, for having given the rooster discrimination to know the difference between day and night."

If we live in the country, we can hear the flesh-and-blood rooster greet the dawn. But if we live in the city, as most of us do, we don't have to be left out—we can attend the dawn celebration in our imagination.

It doesn't matter where we are during sunrise—at home alone, or with our mate, housemates, or families, or already on the subway or bus heading for work. From any of these physical places, our imaginations are free to wander. Our physical bodies may be strap-hanging in a crowded subway train, pressed between lots of other people, but at sunrise our imagined selves can go and take a bath at a hot spring. We can feel the breeze as we emerge from the water, raising our arms, facing the rising sun, opening ourselves to the songs that flow out of us, and blend with the songs of the birds and all the other creatures celebrating the dawn.

You may not be able to see the sunrise with your physical eye. Perhaps you are surrounded by noise. Nevertheless, you can visualize a natural place and visit it in your imagination. In this way, you can hear the rooster and wake into the day.

There are also other ways in which you can make your morning reconnection with the universe. One lies in how you relate to your food: you can eat with consciousness. When you eat an egg for breakfast, don't think of it as coming from the styrofoam box you brought home from the supermarket. Think of the hen that laid it, and the rooster that fertilized the egg which the hen hatched.

When you eat your bowl of corn flakes, devote at least a few seconds to "seeing" the corn—how it grows, with the tassles hanging down; and how the wind sweeps across the cornfield, blowing pollen from one side to the other and making the plants fertile. When you watch this in your imagination, and carry the process from the planted seed up to the present moment in which you are chewing the corn flakes, you see how your eating is connected with the whole fertility dance of the plant world. If we don't become a conscious part of the process, what right have we to eat the corn flakes?

This is why we make a blessing over food before we eat it—to make sure that we eat with consciousness. All of these steps lead us back to the natural universe and into the organic time in which the universe unfolds. The more we live in organic time, the more we are in an appropriate relationship with life.

A MINI-SABBATH AT WORK

Commodity time is the price we pay for organic time. In order to earn a living, this is the bargain you strike: you give your employer work, in return for which he gives you money. While you are working, your time belongs to him, and it's used to create commodities of one sort or another for him. A question arises out of this situation: what is your moral obligation to your employer (what constitutes an honest day's work?) and what is the best way to fulfill it?

In one sense, your obligation is met by accepting the convention of commodity time and acting accordingly while you are at work. The best way to do this, however, and the most productive for your employer, is to step out of commodity time once or twice during the work day to recharge yourself with a hit of organic time. This improves both your sanity and efficiency.

Imagine that it is early or midafternoon. You've already eaten your lunch and digested it. There's a pile of work on your desk, but your energy is low and perhaps you're even feeling a little drowsy. It's time for a coffee break, a chocolate bar, or a handful of nut-raisin-seed mix.

This is a common occurrence; it happens to most people at around the same time of the afternoon. It's the reason that management approved of the afternoon coffee break—it improves workers' efficiency. But there's a better way to do that.

If you can, instead of having a coffee or candy break, find a quiet space where you can sit down, and make Sabbath for ten minutes by allowing your mind to leave the world of *doing* and enter the world of *being*. Your body is aching for this—crying out, "Please let me rest a little bit." I suggest that you spend your afternoon break as a kind of meditation, a moment to say your afternoon prayers. It doesn't need to be long. Ten minutes is really enough. It's better than anything else, and your effectiveness will improve immediately.

A ten-minute cat nap could provide some of the same kind of recharging, but a nap is probably not possible. It *is* possible, though, to place yourself into five minutes of sunset time and five minutes of sunrise time and return yourself to work recycled and refreshed. The exercise I have in mind doesn't even require a special place—you can do it right at your desk.

Sometimes I think we could use an afternoon recycling service to help us out. Imagine that you're working at your desk. It's about two-thirty, and you're running down. It's time for recharging, and since this happens to you on a regular basis, you've arranged to have your service contact you at this time.

Your phone rings, you answer, and the voice on the other end of the line says, "Hello, this is your afternoon recycling service." Now is the time to make yourself truly comfortable. Exhale and take a deep breath which fills your lungs to their capacity. Then exhale again; let it all out until your lungs feel empty. Inhale again, and with the next exhalation, visualize yourself leaning back, back, back, and falling into night. Visualize all the tiredness of your body coming out like a wave, engulfing you, and you yielding to it. Another breath. You slow your pulse even further. At this point you yield wholly to that urge that wants to be rid of work and obligation. Let it encompass you so completely that all that exists is your limp weight on top of the chair leaning against the desk.

Don't forget to breathe. Take another breath. All right. Now you're there. You've fallen into a very relaxed, sleepy state, and one of your favorite images from daydreams or previous meditations comes up again, sustaining and energizing you. Or you relive a peak experience, one of those moments when you *saw*, *felt*, and understood some aspect of your life and its place in the order of the world. Look at that peak experience. Now, in the deepest enjoyment of it, open yourself up again to that verification which comes from the center of the universe. You belong. You are loved. You're integral. You're reborn. You're being nourished. You're growing further.

At this point you're filled with gratefulness. You breathe in once again and with the next breath you feel a zing in the air and you've already turned one hundred and eighty degrees from sunset toward sunrise. Now you're facing a new day and the future. With each breath, you breathe all the way to your toes, then into the bottom of your spine. Your whole body begins to rise, reaching toward what is to come. And here you enter the sunrise, and you open up your concerns for this afternoon, for the rest of the work shift, for the evening you will spend with your family. With each breath you take, you become more and more alert and intent.

You're opening your eyes. You're visualizing your tasks slowly, with ease and focus. You see all the pieces that must fit together and all the steps you have to take. You send out a thank-you to the universe. You look around the room, see all the people in their places, and you acknowledge them. The other person across the room who knows what you have been doing acknowledges you, too. And the voice on your phone says, "Have a good day, Mr. Marvin Doe. I hope to talk to you again tomorrow at the same time. This is your afternoon recycling service. Goodbye."

Marvin Doe returns the phone to its cradle. He doodles for a moment. He has allowed his inner self to send him a picture, which he tacks on the board before him because, by now, he knows that sometime later he will find in it a clue to the matter on which he is working. He is about to continue to work and now he checks his inner monitor.

Ready to go back to work?
Ready.
Ready to invest units of energy?
Ready.
Ready to give attentive awareness?
Ready.
Ready to benefit employer and coworkers?
Ready.
Ready to promote the harmonious well-being of all on this planet?
Ready.
Ready to pursue an optimal level of truth and beauty?
Ready.
Then for God's sake . . .
and Marvin picks up the sheet he last worked on before

the meditation break while he hums, "Behold I am ready and prepared to fulfill the command of my Creator."

FIVE MINUTES OF LEAVE-TAKING

At the end of the work day, we have to take a few steps to separate work from the rest of our day and the rest of our lives. One of the first things to do is to make an inventory of where you stand with your job.

If you take moral issue with the company you work for, you shouldn't be doing that job anyway. Usually you don't have to keep a job if you don't *want* to. But as long as you do it, you have to give something to the job that is righteous and for the good of the company.

Much attention is given to the issues of workers' rights (more pay or safer conditions). Unions exist to address those issues, which is how it should be. But some attention should also be paid to workers' obligations—obligations beyond the level of job descriptions and responsibilities. I'm talking about attitude, good will, conscientiousness, about the desire to do a good job. There is a popular cynicism which holds that since most jobs are not worth doing, they are not worth doing well; that people only do them because they need the money. I'm not arguing with that view. The problem is, it leads to the situation of workers' deriving no satisfaction or sense of accomplishment from their work. They feel they are doing something that is unimportant, second rate, perhaps even harmful. This issue is serious, for it touches the central core of how people feel about themselves.

As you've seen, there are steps the individual can take to derive the most emotional and spiritual nourishment from his or her work. When you unplug from the work day, it is beneficial to assess your performance. In a brief scan, ask yourself the key questions: Did I put in adequate time on my current project? Did I approach it with the right attitude? Did I pay attention? Did I add energy to the office and my coworkers, or was I an energy drain?

When you make a conscious separation from work by spending five minutes at your desk after it's cleaned up, and at least mentally laying out the work for tomorrow, you have put the obligation to your job on the back burner of your mind where it can simmer unattended, yet be ready for your return the next morning.

If you *leave* your work, you don't have to take it home with you. Your subconscious mind will process what has to be processed without your having to consciously sweat over it. During your five minutes of leave-taking, it's a good idea to thank God for the work accomplished: "Now I can leave this work on my desk with the knowledge that I will be ready to handle it tomorrow. I give thanks for what has been achieved today and pray for the strength that will be needed for tomorrow's work."

The concern with doing good work leads us back to another confrontation with God. It is written, "In all thy ways, know Him!" This is the most basic of life duties. Even in the world of work, we have to ask ourselves this question: "Where do I stand in relation to God?"

Before leaving work, look around at your fellow workers and give back some of the blessings you've received. Acts of cooperation or assistance wait to be acknowledged. Also to be acknowledged are interpersonal contacts which may have been negative or irritating. Ask yourself, "What happened today that didn't work out well? Do I have any explanations or apologies to offer my colleagues?" Perhaps you have an unresolved issue with someone due to something that happened during the day. You didn't mention it at the time because you were too busy. Now is the time to approach that person. "Listen," you might say, "I want to go home and relax. I wish you a nice evening, too. But I have to tell you that I didn't appreciate it when you did such-and-such this afternoon. I don't want to make it a major episode, but I was really troubled by how you dealt with me at that time. Rather than carry the irritation and anger home, where it might fester, I'm telling you about it so I can leave it here. This way we both can acknowledge and deal with it, and start fresh with each other tomorrow."

Of course, if you take this kind of interactive step, you need to be willing to be responsible for the flip side. In this instance, you approach the other person and say something like: "I said something to you today that I would not have appreciated if it had been said to me, so I want to let you know I'm sorry. I was under great pressure. Please forgive me. I'm going to make every effort not to let it happen again."

When we treat each other at work as human beings, can you imagine how much easier, more pleasant and productive life in the office or the shop becomes? Another benefit of resolving (or attempting to resolve) interpersonal issues in the workplace and leaving them there is the reduction of the irritation-frustration-anger-violence syndrome in the streets and in our homes. (It is an alarming fact that much of the violence in American life takes place at home between family members. At least part of the cause of this violence can be traced to unresolved frustrations and dissatisfactions brought home from the workplace.)

Always be sure to thank anyone who did something considerate and caring. You can also respond to things you'd postponed earlier, like a request for a piece of information which you put off because you were so preoccupied at the time. Each of these moves adds to the available energy of the group. In an energy crisis, like the one we're in, any energy you can generate is a valuable contribution.

As for coworkers who won't or can't respond, who are stuck in their anger, your effort was not a waste of energy. At the very least, you've cleared out your own system, thus increasing your energy for the next day's work. And there is always the possibility that because of your effort, your reluctant coworker will finally come around and participate in a positive energy exchange.

Some people will never change; they're like black holes sucking up energy and never giving any in return. These people, too, are a part of reality, and there's not much you can do about them except to accommodate them and go about your work as best you can. Recognizing the difference between the possible and the impossible—at work or in any other sphere—defines reality, helping you to make clean-cut separations between one activity and another, so that you are able to act appropriately. Such recognitions keep you on track, whatever sphere of life you happen to be in at any given moment—work or nonwork, fantasy or reality, the days of the week or the Sabbath. Concise separations between one context and another are acts of awareness which maintain your integrity with the organic life of the planet.

DAY IS DONE

When work is done for the day and the door is closed behind you, you are already in transit to your next sphere of action—home. For most people, this is the biggest shift of the day, changing gear from you as worker to you as mate, parent, friend. Perhaps at this point you recall that the Jewish time perception is: "It was evening, it was morning one day"—evening is the beginning of a new day. What happened at the office was yesterday. Turn the page of the calendar in your mind. What will happen at home will be the entrance into the new day. Instead of framing the 9–5 part as the center of your activity, you have made it the end. A new symphony is about to start with your return home.

You are about to reenter the most important sphere in your life, so it is fitting to think about *how* you will do it—in what frame of mind, with what intentions, giving off what vibrations?

In shifting from the work gear to the home gear, your pausing in any one of several neutral places will help make the transition smoother.

There are people who drop by a pub for a drink on their way home. They've done their work for the day, and they give themselves that reward. After a drink or two, they arrive home a little mellower. For some, this is an effective move, but it has its potential dangers. Too many people drink too much at the end of the work day—a quick one becomes a slow three or four. Arriving home tipsy is just as bad as arriving with lots of work worries on your shoulders. Another danger in the pub is the ease with which your focus is distracted—after all, you are pausing for a drink in order to prepare and focus yourself for your reentry into your home space, but drinking can make you more distracted, less in touch.

Other recreational interludes are available. Perhaps there's a museum on the way home, a free or inexpensive one where you can take ten or fifteen minutes to refresh your soul in front of a painting or a piece of sculpture. Maybe there's a park where you can sit on a bench and observe some birds or animals—even the common pigeons and squirrels can put you in touch with the organic pulse of the world. And if there are no animals or birds around, you can connect with plants, which are also living members of our biosphere.

One of the most inspiring things that I've ever seen was a willow tree that had been cut down and made into a telephone pole. The bark had been stripped and the tree soaked in creosote to make it impervious to the weather. Then it was put back in the ground and telephone wires were strung from it. Yet somehow it sprouted roots again, and from the top of the telephone pole new branches began to grow.

There was something so remarkable about it that from time to time on my way home from my office I'd go by to take a look at that tree. It had much to tell me. On the one hand, it gave me an insight. I saw it as a metaphor for the situation of many Jews, Jews who are looking for something more, who feel uprooted, not quite plugged in, but who would really like to sink roots and reach up with branches. On the other hand, pausing to look at that tree— with its tenacity for life that defied all attempts to thwart it—made me feel calm, focused, hopeful. It was a very good frame of mind in which to reenter my home and family life.

Conditions change from time to time and place to place, so it may be that such options are not available to you for your interlude between work and home. But there are other possibilities. While riding home on the bus or subway, you can spend a few minutes reading something you especially enjoy—some favorite poetry, for example. This is an inner interlude which allows you to enter another place in your imagination. And if you are unable even to read for a few minutes, wherever you are you can always take a meditative walk in the garden of your feelings. In some ways, that is the best interlude of all.

* * *

As you approach home, send out an early warning message. Let them know you're coming home and how you feel. "My loved ones, I'm on my way home. Even if there should be some unresolved problem between us at this moment, I still send you the anticipation I feel at coming home to you. I want to be at home. I'm bringing home my love. I'm bringing you the fruits of my labor today. My hope for us is that we have some fun and get restored. I want us to find re-creation together."

This kind of message is a self-fulfilling prophecy. By sending it, you consciously commit yourself to the role of giver. When you walk in the door you will bring energy with you rather than need, complaints, self-pity, and kvetch. Of course you had a hard day. Life is difficult and work is not easy. But complaining never gets you very far. A person in the stage of kvetch usually does not get what he needs, because he is an energy drain. But a person whose needs are coupled with contributions, one who can give as well as take energy, will most likely receive. By sending a positive early warning message to your loved ones at home, you make your intentions clear to yourself, and thus reinforce them. As for your loved ones, if they don't get the message long distance, they will certainly get it the moment you walk through the door.

RELATIONSHIPS: MARRIAGE, DIVORCE, AND REMARRIAGE

From infancy on, we're possessed with the yearning that all our good friends should be under the same covers.

It's a cozy yearning. It says we won't be happy unless everyone we care about comes together in one loving group. As children we feel this yearning very strongly. Later it informs our ideal image of what relationships should be.

MARRIAGE

MARRIAGE AS A SUPPORT SYSTEM FOR THE INCARNATION OF SOULS

The institution of marriage grew out of a biological and, eventually, a cultural necessity. Human beings require an extended growing-up period during which we have to be nourished, taken care of, and taught the things we have to know in order to become functioning members of our species. Hasidism adds the spiritual elements to the definition by saying that marriage is the support system for the incarnation of souls.

The Baal Shem Tov asked why people love children so much. His answer was that a child is a human being who is still very close to his or her conception, and since there was so much ecstasy in the conception, it still shows in the child. As the child grows older, the ecstasy slowly evaporates. But it is a state that the child loves in himself, herself, while it lasts.

Ecstasy facilitates incarnation, in the sense that it is ecstasy that teases a soul into coming to this plane of existence. The teasing is necessary because no soul *wants* to come down here. But it is part of the human process that men and women meet in this lower world, love one another, pass into joy, ecstasy, oneness with one another, and thus cause sparks to emerge. And those sparks attract souls from the higher worlds, which allow themselves to be teased into this world again.

But before passing through the doorway into this reality, the soul wants to be sure that it will be coming to a safe place. It would be a difficult trip to enter this world and not to have a momma and poppa. So it is in the interest of souls temporarily entering this plane of existence that safe places be provided where they can be nurtured, raised, inspired. To fulfill the great and holy purpose for which we are enabled to enter this world, we need a relatively strong intelligence, great awareness, and high consciousness. And we need to make leaps forward from generation (incarnation) to generation—this demands a large brain, which, in turn, needs a slow maturation period. All of this requires a support system into which new beings can be safely born, raised, matured, and enabled to begin that which they have to begin. In practical terms, this support system is based on a bond between a man and a woman, a bond with enough "hassle power" to endure long enough to raise the children, even if it does not last for life. To fill these basic needs, the institution of marriage evolved.

THE RISE AND FALL OF THE INSTITUTION OF MARRIAGE

The institution of marriage has evolved as both more and less than a two-person bond. For most of human history, one did not simply marry an individual, one married into a *family*. And the term *family* (from the root words for household and servant) had a more extended sense: it included kindred or at least the household of parents, children, and servants. When entering a marriage, an individual plugged into a clan network.

Arranging a marriage was a socio-political-economic matter of uniting two clans. It was especially useful as a way of concluding political-military alliances, or at least nonaggression treaties. For instance, we read that King Solomon was termed a king of peace and that he had a thousand wives and concubines; each wife or concubine, however, represented a different political alliance. The harem expressed King Solomon's politics, the politics of peace, not necessarily his attitude toward women.

While it was more than a two-person bond, the institution of marriage was also less. Love was expected to be a footnote, something that developed after the fact, if at all. As it is said of Isaac, he "brought her into his mother Sarah's tent, and took Rebekah, and she became his wife; and he loved her" (Gen. 24:67). Marriage was not contingent upon love, but on how well the clan networks could mesh.

As the song "Do You Love Me?" from *Fiddler on the Roof* points out, the notion of romantic love did not figure in the traditional (Ashkenazi) view of marriage. At most, it was implicit; the explicit notion was of a mutual concern and loyalty.

The institution of marriage, as it evolved, worked well and lasted for a relatively long time because social change and technological innovation were slow. The marriage was embedded in an extended family which dwelt in an inherited house, a physical place rich in the experience of the family. The transmission of tradition was greatly facilitated by the fact that there were three, even four, generations living under one roof.

The striving for separateness and identity between father and son, or mother and daughter, is the ground for a beautiful alliance between grandfather and grandson, or grandmother and granddaughter. The grandparent and grandchild communicate to each other with greater freedom and love than parent and child. Thus, while I rebel against my father's ways and values, I can embrace those of my grandfather lovingly. His God is my God and his ways are my ways. Nowadays, with grandparents out of sight, and frequently out of mind, the transmission is much harder, and we are much poorer culturally.

The nuclear family (papa proton, mama neutron, and a few junior electrons spaced out and speeding around who knows where) is a fragment of the old life-support system of the clan. As a consequence, children of a nuclear family are more prone to fragmentation of personality. To compensate for this alienation, there is a very great yearning among us for oneness and belonging. (This yearning is increasingly exploited by economic and political hucksters, who use an image of that cozy, warm family to make us buy breakfast cereal or vote for Candidate X.)

It is very hard for the nuclear family to remain intact.

The stresses on it are immense; it takes people of great stability to be able to hold it together, and such stability is usually achieved at the price of consciousness. But if awareness is inversely related to stability, then a more conscious family unit will be less stable, and that puts the support system for nurturing children at risk. Since the evolution and, ultimately, the survival of the planet depend upon increased consciousness, we must attempt to replicate the stability of the traditional *organic* family. (If we extend this metaphor, the nuclear family can be seen as a product of the decomposition and decay of the healthy organic family.)

Of course, in our search for solutions, we can't go back. We will have to devise extended quasi-families, large enough to achieve stability as a whole despite the instability of individual couplings. In a Jewish context, the Havura movement, mentioned earlier, can be seen as a small step in this direction.*

THE *KETUBA* AND THE MARRIAGE COVENANT

The *ketuba*, the traditional Jewish marriage contract, was instituted at the time of the Babylonian exile (second century B.C.E.). It guarantees standard sums of money for

*The National Havurah Coordinating Committee serves as an educational resource and networking center for Havurot in America and Canada. It fosters their development through national, regional, and local conferences; through institutes for intensive Jewish study; through its quarterly newsletter, *Havurah*; and through program ideas, study aids, and other resources.

For further information about Havurot in your community or the programs of the NHCC, please write to:

The National Havurah Coordinating Committee
31 E. 28 St.
New York 10011 or call: (212) 889-9080

the wife upon the termination of the relationship by divorce or death. As long as inheritance was legally transferred only from father to son, bypassing the wife, the *ketuba* represented a relatively progressive idea: it mandated that a widowed wife should not be left destitute if her husband had not been destitute. But today, we strive for a condition in which the economic survival of ex-wives is not dependent on the largesse of sons or husbands. And the covenant which two people make when they marry is quite different.

The Baal Shem Tov said that if a couple finds there is a lack of harmony in their marriage, they should read the *ketuba* aloud, together. The thought behind this teaching is that such an act would remanifest the juice and energy involved in the original covenant, as expressed by the *ketuba*. There is power in this teaching because it is at the moment of making such a covenant that two people come together with the greatest energy, energy that can propel them toward each other, and toward harmony with the One. In its highest form, the *ketuba* can and should be a continuing source of energy.

THE MARRIAGE CEREMONY

When I served as a rabbi to congregations, engaged couples would frequently ask me for the quickest possible ceremony. I thought they were very shortsighted, because they were implicitly asking to be wedded together in the weakest way, and thus for the briefest "acceptable" marriage. My role was to help aim them toward forever, yet they were counting the minutes of the ceremony. In so doing, they were shortchanging themselves.

If a couple gets a quickie marriage, is the fifteen minutes of that abbreviated ceremony enough time in which to transmit all the energy they will need throughout their life together, so that they will be able to work through the problems that are bound to arise and still come back toward each other and toward the One? Common sense tells us the answer is probably no.

One part of the traditional ceremony is called "veiling the bride." Before she approaches the canopy under which the ceremony will take place, the bride's face is covered with a veil. At one point during the ceremony, the groom symbolically must determine that the woman before him is really his bride and that he intends to marry her, so he looks at her face. I would like to suggest another, deeper level of significance and intention (kavanah) associated with this ritual.

Before the bride is veiled, the bride and groom should sit facing one another, looking into each other's souls in such a way that they see not only the love, sweetness, and understanding, but also the craziness, ugliness, and angers. In short, each should see the whole range of attributes in the other, and ask him- or herself, "Can I say yes to that?"

This is a mutual introspection. Each must contact the enlightened being in the other and ask, "Do I think this union will be good for me? Will it lead to a greater, richer, deeper life, or will it be destructive? Will it take a whole series of incarnations later on to get me out of what this wedding will get me into?"

If the bride and groom have encountered each other and given consent to the union with their highest selves, then the officiating officer may say, "By the authority vested in me, I hereby declare you to be man and wife," because authority has now been given from that place where authority resides—the domain of higher selves. So the ceremony of veiling the bride may function, on a deeper level, as an affirmation of the marriage covenant, a sort of esoteric signing of the marriage contract.

In the sphere of legalisms, the ketuba is a contract, a legal document, and legal documents should be read by lawyers before they are signed. In the sphere of souls, the ketuba is a covenant, and covenants are ratified by the coming together of enlightened souls. This may happen even before the legal marriage ceremony. Frequently, however, it doesn't happen at all, and then all that the marriage ceremony welds together are legal living arrangements. But if it does happen, then the couple has something very strong that either or both can invoke during the rough stretches of the marriage. A pledge given by one's highest self is real; it can be ignored, but not denied.

The wedding ceremony must also involve the guests, and involve them in a meaningful way. In effect, they should be asked, "People, what's the best energy you can give to this couple at this moment, so that life, holiness, awareness, and love, and all the 'juice' that comes from God can be theirs? Through this ceremony, you may deposit for them whatever you have to give them for their life together." So the ceremony must be such that it helps the guests, as well as the couple and the bridal party, call upon their highest selves.

PREMARITAL EXPERIENCE

There is no point denying reality. This is true for everyone, but especially for those of us who are committed to an empirical approach to life and religion. As we see it, the real conditions and concerns of our lives have to be addressed by our religious practices. If they are not, religion itself diminishes in significance.

The sexual revolution that has occurred in America and most of the Western world has brought about major changes in the ways people relate to and live with each other. And this revolution is by no means over. The backlash, typified by the fundamentalist right and the "moral majority," is an individual wave in a tide that has already turned. The role of women, for example, continues to evolve in the direction of greater participation and toward the goal of self-determination.

We have gone beyond the day when the majority of women would silently settle for the role of housewife to the exclusion of all other possibilities. In recent years, this change has been one of the greatest sources of energy in our society. The effect of "woman power" on the texture of Western civilization has been so profound, it makes us wonder what the effect will be when the women of Islam flower forth with all their beautiful strength.

Within our own Jewish world, we have already seen some of the results of women's changing expectations. In more and more congregations, women are demanding and winning the right to greater participation. As mentioned earlier, the original Havura was established on the basis of sexual equality—it was obvious to everyone involved that women would be equal members of the group and participate fully as leaders. And most exciting of all—over the past few years, several women have been ordained as Rabbis. The problem is, however, that many women were turned off by the limitations and restrictions placed on them by earlier concepts and practices, and many of these women remain turned off. Speaking directly to women in this category, I'd like to say that Judaism *can* respond to your needs and to the realities of your lives. Judaism *can* nourish you and provide the context in which you can become your greatest self. At the 1981 Havura conference, a committee on women's liturgy was established for the specific purpose of creating prayers which speak directly to the needs of women.

Women's liberation and the sexual revolution are aspects of the same phenomenon, a major shift in perspective and attitude that has changed the landscape of human relationships. Expectations, definitions, and processes have altered. For example, the traditional *ketuba* (marriage contract) rests on several assumptions, one of which is that the bride be a virgin. There was a time when this assumption was usually valid. The mores and customs of another era were such that women's sexual behavior was closely controlled by society (*men*). Deviations, when discovered among "respectable" women, were cause for punishment and social stigma. Today, however, there are no such total, all-encompassing controls.

Sex before marriage is no longer perceived by most people as a cause for shame or social disgrace. In fact, it is increasingly common for couples to openly live together before they are married, in a unique kind of relationship that is more than "going steady" or being engaged, but is less than marriage, with its greater commitment.

Though it is by no means always the case, living together frequently serves as a prelude to marriage. When couples who have been living together ask me to perform their wedding ceremony, I generally find that they have already worked through much of the interpersonal material that has to be dealt with if a solid marriage is to follow.

A happy marriage is like a maple tree—its roots go deep, its branches reach to heaven, its sweet sap rises even in the winter, its leaves glow more warmly as the year passes, it is very strong, and it lives a long time. But unlike the maple, a marriage needs constant care and attention. Love is the indispensable ingredient in a marriage, but there must also be goodwill, clear-sightedness, compatibility, sharing, concern, commitment, and perhaps most of all, a willingness on the part of each partner to work hard.

Marriage is not easy in our day and age. The success rate has been dropping steadily for years. Along with crime and inflation, divorce is one of the big three rising rates. With these harsh realities in mind, I frequently have apprehensions and even reservations when I'm asked to marry a couple who has not lived together. Marriage must be taken very seriously, which is difficult to do until the couple has had experience with each other. Part of approaching marriage seriously has to do with asking the right questions, agreeing on definitions, and synchronizing expectations. More often than not, the experience of living together before marriage provides the shared context out of which can emerge those questions, definitions, and expectations.

As part of performing a wedding, I meet with the couple beforehand and offer my counseling services. In these discussions I ask straightforward questions about their *intentions* and *expectations*. I do not limit myself to the legalistic text of the marriage contract which, after all, is an external and general document. I focus instead on the internal and particular: "What do you intend to give to this marriage, and what do you expect to get from it? With what strength do you expect to hold to your intentions? What do you really want to negotiate with your mate?"

These questions must be asked even if serious reconsideration leads to the dissolution of the relationship.

CHANGES AND RENEWALS

At the end of the classic fairy tale, after the lovers have been reunited, there is usually the familiar line, "and they lived happily ever after." It sounds good but it's clearly make-believe, because it presents a static model of marriage. The implication is that after the current problem is solved, whatever it is, no other problem will ever arise again. The truth is more demanding—in this world, we and our relationships are always in process, always in the act of happening. It is just when a marriage becomes static, when the interactions and exchanges grind to a halt, that the marriage is in the greatest trouble.

A good marriage requires hard work, much of it directed to the process of sharing feelings and ideas. When this process falters and the lines of communication close down, it is urgent that they be reopened. Sometimes this is made particularly difficult by the fact that the husband and wife are out of phase with each other, operating on different frequencies. The marriage of a deliberate, planning person to a spontaneous ad-hoc person is one example of such a mismatch. Differences in diet can profoundly affect a marriage; so can sleeping habits. Such situations can be painful and confusing. Until the cause of dysfunction is known, genuine communication can't resume, even with the good will of both parties. A common though frequently ignored source of this problem is the cyclical nature of marriage.

Everything in this world is subject to periodicity. In God's creation, nothing stands still. Even the Divine Attributes are revealed in cycles and over time.

The metaphysics of Jewish mysticism defines ten Divine Attributes (sefirot), seven of which are manifest in this world: grace, strength, beauty, victory, glory, foundation, and kingdom. These Divine Attributes flow through all phenomena, including marriages. Traditionally, they reveal themselves sequentially, each for a year, giving rise to seven-year cycles.*

---

*Units of seven are common in the periodicity of nature, and certainly apply to marriage. But the complexity of life is such that other time cycles are in effect concurrently. The interpersonal phenomena discussed here (growth, change, loss of synchronicity) may surface in a marriage at any time. Whenever they do, they should be recognized and dealt with.

All marriages are potentially subject to the "seven year itch" or "hitch," as the case may be. This happens at the end of each seven-year cycle, when a jump—a sort of quantum leap—has to be made to the next cycle. The purpose of this periodic leap is to avoid stasis and stagnation, to keep things dynamic. The "itch" is not an ailment; it is nature's way of insuring forward movement.

This movement is not accurately described by the word *cycle*. A cycle is relatively static; its motion is confined to one plane. Since nothing natural is static, the process is more accurately characterized as a helicycle, an upwardly turning spiral. The second seven-year period of a marriage, for instance, is not a return to the first seven years, though one is certain to find similarities and analogies.

When a helicycle of a marriage is about to end, and before or as the next helicycle starts, there is the in-between time when the itch of growth and change demands attention. Each of the partners has experienced a reshaping, which in and of itself calls for readjustments in the relationship. But the problem is compounded when the rate of direction of change experienced by one partner is markedly different than that of the other. This is the circumstance which frequently throws husband and wife out of phase and undermines communication. The same words may be spoken as before, but the points of view have changed and the meanings of the words are probably different.

Within the intensity of the relationship, each partner has helped the other to become more himself or herself. Because of this, they look at each other in a new way. Questions arise, tensions mount, and there is pressure to renegotiate some of the basic assumptions underlying the relationship.

When it is possible (and occasionally it is), I like to invite couples back seven years after their wedding and perform a ceremony which is aimed at helping them renegotiate and reaffirm the covenant between them. After all, they are not the same people they were earlier.

The design and content of this renewal ceremony is still evolving, but an essential feature is a reexamination of each partner's goals and priorities, which in all probability have changed in some way. Another vital area is expectations—what are their current expectations of each other and the relationship?

In all likelihood, many individual details or components of the relationship have also changed. In addition to the emotional, intellectual, and spiritual changes experienced by each partner, there are the evolving external realities of a marriage, such as children, careers, finances, health, and so on.

When such changes are not dealt with in an honest, open way, the result is tension. All the energies in the marriage are not pulling in the same direction with the same effort, so there is strain. When the tension is great enough, the couple's central commitment to each other is stretched to the breaking point. All relationships do not have to reach this precarious position, but when they do, there are ways of alleviating the strain.

The cause of such strain lies in a common habit: our responding to a new situation without pausing to consciously recognize it for what it is. Instead, we make quick adjustments, give up something here or there, take on a little more responsibility in the household, and keep the trip going. The adjustments are not usually talked about; we just do them as part of the business of living our lives.

But unless we consciously look at the changes that have occurred, and openly and seriously discuss the readjustments that will have to be made, resentments and anger frequently grow, consciously or unconsciously. We go through the motions so that it looks as if we are leading our lives, but really our lives are leading us.

Sometimes within a marriage we can lose sight of our own selves. For this reason, I think it is a good idea to invite people close to the couple to come in for the renewal ceremony and help out as "witnesses" and loving friends. These people can provide a multifaceted mirror in which the couple can see themselves from new points of view and assess their relationship in a fresh way. The great advantage of this network approach is the consciousness and concern it brings forth.

In truth, we do not yet know with any great certainty how to work out the issues that can injure or destroy marriages. I'm not talking about the ones that permeate impossible relationships—those thoroughly painful marriages that seem doomed from the start and only grow worse with time. Rather, I mean those issues that *can* be discussed and negotiated, issues that may be painful but not terminal. Often people don't know the difference, and give up on a relationship when they should invest more energy in it.

Still, I see reason for hope. Coming over the horizon for the last decade or two has been a promising wave of people-helping ideas and practices—humanistic and transpersonal psychologies, for example, and family therapy, support groups, Havurot, and a growing longing among people for a spiritual element of life. The focus of these tools has moved from emergency intervention (in cases of pathology) to the goal of an increase of well-being and a rise in energy and joy. It seems to me that all these techniques have to be explored in our attempts to create strong and supple marriages.

THE VARIETY OF
INTIMATE EXPERIENCE

We have scarcely begun our conceptual map of marriage. What we have so far is an incomplete outline of the general area and many specific sections marked "unexplored territory." Some of the things to reflect on are:

Timing. When do couples set aside time to be together in an intimate way? Usually at the end of the day, after everything else in their lives has been taken care of—work, the children, cleaning up after the evening meal, social obligations, reading, watching television. Almost anything at all seems to be given priority over intimacy.

As soon as you think about it, it's obvious that the priorities are upside-down. The relationship in our lives which should receive the freshest and greatest energy receives the least. Everybody with whom we have had contact during the day (at work, and so on) receives better energy than does the person with whom we have chosen to share our lives.

The Sacrament of Sexual Intimacy. In the loving cosmogony of Reb Hayim Haikel, an eighteenth century Hasidic master, "Creation was for the purpose of lovemaking. As long as their was only one-ness, there was no delight. But when division occurred and afterwards they [man and woman] were connected with one another, this brought about great delight." For the wisest and most elevated among us, every carnal thought leads to God. The rest of us must strive toward this goal.

We speak of sex as a sacrament in which we offer up ourselves to each other. But what *is* the sacramental element in it? How do the actions of our bodies become offerings to God? A physical act must be somehow spiritualized to become sacramental. Our conscious intentions are at the heart of the matter, but we have to think about what exactly spiritualized foreplay would be, to lead into intercourse as sacrament.

Interpersonal Intimacy. The partners in a relationship serve many functions for each other. One of the most important is to be a mirror in which we give the other a reflection of her- or himself. Of course, this raises questions. When does the reflecting of unpleasant truth lead to friction and when does this friction lead to a higher harmony? And, further, what service is performed by the friction?

Among Jewish mystics, it is commonly thought that discord occurs in the shadow of spirituality. It is further held that discord cannot be an essential part of the spiritual dialectic and that when we argue, the Divine is not present. This raises the obvious question: Is the Divine present in phony harmony, in those instances in which we pretend with each other in order to create a false facade in the name of peace?

Our own experience provides the answer to this question, and it is just the opposite. It is precisely in the instances of phony harmony that we feel most alienated from each other and from God, that we feel the Divine truly is *not* present. Phoniness seems to be the one state of being in which we can't say, "Whatever is happening is what is supposed to happen."

Phoniness is a negative space, an entropic state in which nothing productive can take place. Phony harmony is profaned deadlock. Holy wedlock, on the other hand, by its very definition, must include a mutual reflecting of truth between the partners. This, as we all know, creates the potential for hassles. However painful, and wherever they may lead, truthful hassles are better than phony harmony.

A word of caution: there *is* such a thing as indiscriminate or vindictive feedback, those reflections of ours that are harmful to our mates. Perhaps a specific piece of feedback is not true because it has been distorted by our own needs, or perhaps our mate is not ready to deal with the particular truth we are reflecting at a given moment. We could do well to establish some guidelines to help us decide when a reflection will advance the harmony of our union (even when the advance is not immediate), and when it will actually be a disservice. Since all relationships are unique in the texture of their being, we must each find our own guidelines based on the particular realities of the situation. Introspection and increased self-awareness are the necessary first steps.

DIVORCE

MADE IN HEAVEN, BROKEN IN HELL

However a marriage begins, it may deteriorate into a tragedy of manners, a kind of poker game in which each player plays as close to the vest as possible. The light of love and unity fades, and in the darkness each player goes through the motions without tipping his or her hand.

At night the man and woman might still lie side by side, but their minds are shielded from each other. One or both may set up opaque barriers to hide little lies, or to prevent the other from asking for things that one no longer wants or dares to give.

The relationship is made obscure by a self-willed smokescreen which hides the "partners" from each other and even blocks the little crack of light under the door of their hearts which might tell the other that he or she is still at home.

Empathy, rapport, and telepathy—all sorts of nonverbal communications of "what's for real"—are shut off; things deteriorate from the perfect attunement that brought two people together at just the right time to a situation where neither really hears what the other is saying. One or both feels, "Since I no longer want to live up to your expectations, and I can't stand to argue under such a circumstance, I will myself to become opaque." For their own good, both have to learn to recognize and deal with that opaqueness; everybody can get hurt in the dark.

CLIMBING OUT OF THE PIT

A marriage takes a lot of goodwill, a lot of energy and highly-charged batteries to hold itself together. But what happens when the goodwill is gone? What happens when a person feels the marriage is a bottomless pit and doesn't want to pour in any more energy, even if he or she has it? What happens when one wants to say, "I'm sorry, there simply is no more. It would take more energy than I can afford, and you can't squeeze energy from a stone."

What happens during such a marital energy crisis is chaos. Everything falls apart. The drain widens and everybody loses more and more energy. Husband and wife no longer agree on anything. Children witness and absorb daily battles or bitter silence. A black cloud lies over the whole family. Negative momentum sends everything careening downward and outward in a crazy spiral. The result is fragmentation, emotional isolation in which husband and wife seek every opportunity not to be with each other.

In the midst of this worsening situation, there may be temporary truces. And in view of the alternatives, a dying marriage may be (or may seem to be) a convenient situation, better than a furnished room, restaurant meals, and one night stands. But if this kind of shortsighted convenience is all that's left in a marriage, a person has to be at least half unconscious to even pretend that it's tolerable.

It's very hard to sustain any level of relationship if you're only halfway conscious. You still want to stay open to the One and to the One-ing, to the Heart, to Truth, to God, to all the things of higher value, but if your marriage has degenerated and then rigidified into one of inconvenience, it simply won't work. If there's no goodwill, you can't even fall back on allegiance, because the real basis for such allegiance has eroded.

But how do you know you're in the inescapable pit, that you've reached rock bottom and are not just on the down-swing of a phase? This is a terrible question to have to encounter because the answer is: you never know. You never know with certainty. But often, when things get bad enough, one or both of the partners get the feeling that if they don't break free of the relationship, they will become permanently bent out of shape and bend the other as well. Such feelings should not be ignored.

Some relationships get so bad, they rip people apart. Ego battering can continue relentlessly until there's no ego left. When the ego is destroyed, it's hard, if not impossible, to deal with the world on any level. So in the name of self-preservation, and for the sake of the partner, who is still first of all a human being, destructive marriages should not be allowed to destroy—they should be ended.

There is another Hasidic viewpoint on this matter which states that if you're married to someone, you'd better stay and work it out. If not, you'll have to do it again in the next incarnation, so you might as well see it through to the end. However, the dynamic pattern of the couple's interaction may be such that even in a whole lifetime, all the couple could ever give each other is hell.

Some might say that anything not worked out in a first marriage will corrupt the next marriage and have to be worked out there. There certainly is a great deal to be gained from a post-mortem of a failed relationship: some people learn from the first time, so the second time around they have a different kind of marriage. They've asked themselves some of the necessary questions and have examined and modified their habitual response to persons of the opposite sex. They have found the bedrock of their value system on which they can build their next relationship and heal their battered self-esteem. Since divorce is major surgery of one's social being, gentle convalescing is often necessary before one enters into new relationships.

DIVORCE, JEWISH STYLE

According to Jewish law, divorce is essentially no-fault—not an antagonistic procedure between advocates (lawyers) for the two parties. This is because the divorce settlement is specified before the marriage, in the ketuba. But besides being no-fault, divorce must be consensual; both parties must collaboratively come to the rabbi to freely release each other. To do that, a good deal of work must come before the actual divorce.

A religious divorce is the last step; it may be preceded by a civil separation, even a legal (state) divorce.

The procedure for Jewish divorce is as follows: The couple approaches the rabbi and ask him to divorce them. He then asks them to appear before him together. The husband must then empower a scribe to write a document of divorce, freeing his wife to marry or not marry any man she chooses, no strings attached. The rabbi determines that the wife is really willing to take the divorce and is not doing so under coercion. (Since the divorce must return total freedom to the wife, all areas of dispute—custody, visitation, and so on—are best worked out before the religious document of divorce can be written.) The scribe then writes the document and two witnesses sign it. Then the husband takes it, hands it to his wife, who takes it, puts it under her arm, and walks out of the room—symbolizing that she now has full freedom to go anywhere she wants. When she comes back into the room, the witnesses check the document to ensure that the document they saw the husband hand to her really is a bill of divorce. The scribe confirms that it is the bill of divorce he wrote, and the witnesses confirm to the rabbi that it is the document they signed. Then the husband states that of his own free will, he empowered the scribe to write it. When all that's established, the rabbi takes the bill of divorce, folds it, and cuts through it (like perforating a cancelled check) and that's that; they're divorced. By Halachic law, the woman is not permitted to remarry for three months afterwards, to remove any doubt about the paternity of a subsequent child, and a kohen (one of priestly descent) can't marry a divorcee; other than that, she's perfectly free.

At this point, you may feel a rise of anger at Jewish law for being so patriarchal in this day and age. Such anger can fuel the process necessary to right the remaining wrongs. Making marriage equitable and more functional will require, of necessity, a rabbinate composed of men and women.

The above is a quick run-through of the external, legalistic phenomenology of Jewish divorce. But what about

the internal? Here, the task is to get the couple to agree
and work for their mutual benefit, even though they have
just come through hell together. In my own work with
divorcing couples, I ask the wife to look the husband in
the eye the same way she looked at him before they got
married, with the same concern and say, "For the benefit
of both of us, I give you complete release from my expectations of you and involvement in your life. Let's really let
go of each other, let's not have any more hooks or things to
play out with the kids." Then I ask the husband to do the
same. At this point, if there are children in the marriage, I
point out to the couple that it is only their relationship as
husband and wife that is touched by the divorce, and that
they will remain as coparents forever. Hence, they must
make provisions so that they will be able to function for
the benefit of the children.

I usually ask a couple to write each other letters in
which they say the truths that they hadn't been able to tell
each other during the marriage. After they've read each
other's letters, we burn them; they do not need more
evidence of the failure of the marriage.

Then I ask each to offer the other a dollar bill, as
settlement in full of all remaining debts from the marriage—financial debts, social debts, emotional debts—and
if either feels that's not enough restitution, they need more
negotiation; otherwise, they've settled the ketuba.

And, finally, when each can really let the other go, if I
have some schnapps around and if they're into drinking, I
ask them to drink each other a l'chaim (a toast to life) so
that they can send each other off with good wishes: You go
to your life, I'm off to mine, and may God bless us.

When a divorce is over, people must face the fact that
something has died. It seems like an obvious thing to do,

but somehow in their anger or pain some people never get around to it. So I remind people to mourn. I ask each partner to make a three-day retreat to mourn for the relationship. Until it is properly mourned, a relationship won't be given up and dropped. If it's not mourned, it becomes part of the unnecessary baggage the two lug around, unneeded dirt to clutter up their other relationships.

Divorce is, alas, a fact of our existence. We must confront it. When we think it's inappropriate, we should try to prevent it by helping the couple work it out. But when everything fails and divorce is inevitable, we must try to make it as meaningful as possible. In the end, we must learn to spiritualize divorce—as strange as that may sound. Divorce should restore to each person the ability to continue heading back toward God and an at-one-ment with the universe. It should also release them to find in themselves what they didn't find in the other.

REMARRIAGE

This section will, alas, be short, not because there are few instances of remarriage, but because we have not yet paid enough attention to this particularly sensitive kind of wedding. We have centuries of tradition and experience to draw on when performing a marriage between two fresh and relatively innocent people who are marrying for the first time, but until now we have shunned and scarcely begun to think of the unique needs (ceremonial, psychological, and spiritual) of people who have already been through a marriage and divorce.

In our prepackaged, instant-relief world, we are urged by the mass media to believe that speed is the highest virtue. Quickie marriages, followed by quickie divorces, are presented as the new American norm. Our painful divorce statistics tend to bear this out, but too often we blind ourselves to the cause-and-effect relationship. Quickie marriages are a *cause* of quickie divorce, and quickie divorces, in turn, are a cause for failure in the next marriage. So when a couple asks me to perform their wedding, and one or both of them have been divorced, I try to address their needs.

The first thing to do is slow them down and examine their state of mind. Is the earlier marriage truly over? Is it done with and laid to rest, or is it still an active force in their lives? If either or both of them have not observed a mourning period for the dead marriage, I ask them to do so. Usually this is a harrowing experience, because it reopens wounds that have not yet completely healed. But if it is done with a high degree of conscious intention, it acts as a disinfecting process and allows the wounds to finally heal properly.

Divorced people enter a new marriage with a set of expectations that have been shaped, to one degree or another, by their earlier marriage. These expectations must be discussed as openly as possible, and so should areas of vulnerability.

Sometimes this examination process works remarkably well because the couple (one or both) have learned and profited from the earlier marriage, despite the pain and disappointment. At other times, the ghost of the earlier marriage cannot be laid to rest, and it haunts the new relationship into another failure. And then, too, there are the personal issues, problems which may have caused the earlier failure and which have not yet been worked out. As I suggested earlier, there is much work to be done in the area of remarriage, particularly since it appears to be a continually growing phenomenon.

Other areas of concern that need to be addressed include:

—The role of the children (if there are any) in the ceremony. Their participation and involvement must be as meaningful as possible, for they have as much at stake as anybody. Time and place must be made for them to express their feelings—fears, pain, hopes, and expectations.

—The role of the ex-mate, if caring and concerned support can be expected.

—The role of the former in-laws. After all, just because someone legally ceases to be a relative after a divorce does not negate the years of familial and emotional involvement.

Perhaps when enough people have given thought and energy to the issue of remarriage, a new or redesigned ceremony will evolve that can serve a set of very special needs.

THE TEACHINGS
OF THE BODY

OUR BODIES ARE ALSO FOR GOD

Among those who seek spiritual enlightenment, there are two distinct attitudes toward the body. One view is that the body is a hindrance, an obstacle we must overcome in order to release our spirits. This view leads quite logically to denial of the body, to fasting and mortification, in an attempt to override the demands of the flesh. Body and spirit are seen as separate and conflicting entities.

The other view, which sees the body as a natural part of our beings, is a fundamental tenet of Hasidism. The distinctions between body and spirit are acknowledged, but the nature of the relationship is seen as cooperative and unifying. The joys of the body enhance the joys of the soul. When the body dances, the soul claps her hands.

FROM MY FLESH I SEE GOD

The Baal Shem Tov once said, "Even if you are free from sin, when your body is not strong, your soul will be too weak to serve God in the proper way."

Years later, his great-grandson, Reb Nachman of Bratzlav, offered the following teaching on Rosh Hashanah. It concerns the blowing of the *shofar* (hollowed ram's horn) at the end of the service, and the power that sound has to snap our beings (soul and body) into clear focus. Reb Nachman (who died in 1810) amplifies the importance his great-grandfather placed on our bodies, and foreshadows our contemporary understanding of the reciprocal holistic relationship between mind and body and the phenomenon now known as biofeedback.

Said Reb Nachman, "Each person needs to have genuine compassion for his body, for its very flesh, and to share with it all the enlightenments of the soul. But this can happen only when the body is ready. So we must prepare our bodies by composing them and making them clear. When this is done, and the body is lucid and focused, it is able to receive and absorb the soul's enlightenment."

Sometimes the soul slips and falls from her rung. If the body is clear and luminous, focused and in harmony within itself, the soul can use it to raise herself back to her rung. She can ride on the body's delights in its own energy, and so remember her own delights and reascend to them. Besides, the body remembers all the light it received from the soul which she shared with it at other times, and in turn reflects it back to the soul. In these ways, the soul can use the body's ecstasy to recapture her own.

"Thus the words of Job: *From my flesh shall I see God.*"*

---

*This teaching was transmitted to me by the late, sainted Reb Gedaliah Kenig of Safed.

FIRST THINGS FIRST

You are the instrument on which God plays. It is vital that you are tuned correctly. When you are, the Spirit of God can rest on you and the music will flow sweetly. If you're out of tune when you present yourself to God, all the music that follows will be off-key, sour, and not quite right.

As in all things, when we intend to do spiritual work, we must begin at the beginning. In any of our preparations before attempting spiritual work, much of the emphasis should be on getting our bodies ready to pray in a manner that is appropriate. When asked by a Hasid what he does before praying, the Tzanzer Rebbe replied, "I pray that I might be able to pray properly!"

The importance of the body and body preparation is also seen clearly in the morning prayer service, which begins with such prayers as:

"Blessed are You, Lord our God, King of the Universe, Who opens the eyes of the blind. . . . who straightens the bowed. . . . who gives strength to the weary. . . . who clothes the naked."

Each of these blessings concerns our bodies.

TUNING IN TO YOUR BODY*

Our bodies have messages for us to which we are frequently deaf. When we experience physical pain, we usually take an aspirin. We respond to the messages of body

*For teaching me focusing and for his ideas, I'm in debt to Dr. Eugene Gendlin of the University of Chicago, author of Focusing.

pain as if they had no meaning other than unpleasant physical sensation. The impulse transmitted along our nervous system flashes 'ache in the left shoulder' or 'pain in the right side,' and we take a pill.

But the physical sensations are only the vehicles of the message—the attention-getters. We take aspirin to block the pain, but we also block the message the body is sending to our awareness. When Reb Nachman advises us to clear our bodies, he means that we should take care of them, attend to the basic needs all living bodies have. Then we can achieve a state of physical well-being which is a precondition to clear communication between our bodies and our spiritual awareness.

The messages sent by the body do not come in words; they come as a kind of feeling, a deep body sense. When your body is clear and in a state of well-being, you are able to focus your entire self (soul and body) in the present tense, in this very moment. The process of focusing is a way of saying "Here I am—I am here." You are saying this to yourself, to God and His universe, but not in words. You are saying it on all the wavelengths of your being.

BASIC NEEDS

When you are hungry and tired or have an urgent need to go to the toilet while driving home, the messages sent by your body are very insistent. In fact, the messages are like screaming babies: Feed Me! Let Me Rest! Take Me To The Toilet!

At moments like these, it is sometimes difficult to see the connections between your body and your soul. Nevertheless, they are there. Taking care of the screaming babies inside you is the first step on the ladder to spiritual ecstasy. That is only right; it is the natural order of the universe: attend to basic things first, and higher things will follow.

When the body is hungry, you feed it. Jewish law calls for a prayer of thanksgiving. There is a verse which is usually translated, "You will eat, you will be satisfied, and it will be your duty to give thanks." But Reb Shneur Zalman of Ladi translated it this way: "If you will eat, and you will pay attention to your eating [not that the robot in you will eat, but that you will eat with consciousness] and you will be satisfied, it will follow *normally* that you will offer your blessing."

He saw the blessing as a step in a natural progression of related events, as part of the same process which included the eating. He saw the unity, and stressed the inter-connectedness of individual events. This too is an aspect of well-being.

The point of Reb Shneur Zalman's translation, in terms of your spiritual pursuit, is this: when basic needs are met, and met with awareness and whole-heartedness, the likelihood is that you can climb the spiritual ladder. If, however, you attempt to climb the ladder before reaching the condition of well-being, there will be problems.

Awareness of your actual body experience is one of the most important keys to spiritual work. Windows to this awareness are built into the tradition. For example, after you go to the toilet and relieve yourself, there is a blessing for the successful completion of this most elementary and necessary act: "I worship you God. You are a cosmic God. You made me with passage and duct, vein and orifice. You made me wisely. If one of those were clogged, or if it seeped and leaked, I could not live and breathe, eat, or eliminate. In less than an hour I would be dead. So when it all works right, I am amazed at your goodness and your wisdom. And I worship you, Healer of my body, amazing us with daily wonders."

From this blessing, you get a sense of the body's involvement in spiritual work and its role in the natural processes of the universe. Usually, however, this blessing is refined in translation. Its subject matter—the orifices of your body and their functions—is considered offensive and even indecent by some people, so they have edited the translation until you don't know what you are actually reciting: "Blessed is our Eternal God, Creator of the Universe, who has made our bodies with wisdom, combining veins, arteries, and vital organs into a finely balanced network. Wondrous Fashioner and Sustainer of Life, Source of our health and strength, we give You thanks and praise."

When this prayer is made so 'inoffensive' and the real meaning has been bleached out, you don't check your body against it. And if your body is not in a state of thanksgiving for the smooth operation of its most basic function, genuine prayer and spiritual ascent do not flow freely.

There is another attitude toward the body that should be mentioned in this context, and it concerns the things we do to ourselves, things we'd never take from anyone else. I'm referring to the way some of us push ourselves through the day, allowing the taskmaster inside to drive us from one task to the next, with no sense of rest, even when we eat.

I'm also thinking about the junk foods we inflict on our bodies, the cigarettes, the chemical additives, things that harm our bodies instead of healing and helping them. If somebody else drove you through the day at that ulcer-inducing pace, or *forced* you to smoke cigarettes or eat junk food, you wouldn't stand for it. "I'm not a slave!"

you'd say. "What right do you have to do that to me? God redeemed me from the house of bondage and He redeems me every day." And yet we drive ourselves and harm ourselves all the time.

The recognition that it is a *mitzvah* (good deed) to take care of the vehicle which is the body should be one of your first recognitions. For this reason, we must stress again that any work done in the area of your spiritual consciousness *must* be preceded by care of the body. If not, your path becomes dangerous, because you are ignoring and overriding body signals. It's like driving your car when the oil pressure signal flashes red: the car *seems* all right, but you are burning out the engine.

If your way of doing things allows you to override your body signals, you are very likely going to override the signals of the heart and of the mind. It is best to break this pattern as early as possible at the level of the body.

So tune in to your body. Listen to it. It comes from God and is one of the ways that lead back to Him.

GETTING THE MESSAGE

Our intentions, imagination, and spiritual energies are best focused when the body has been attended to—fed, washed, groomed, repaired, and cared for. As Reb Nachman suggested, the body has to be tuned up so that it runs smoothly on its own energy. All the parts have to be in working order, each separately and also in the way they interact.

Many aspects of body care and maintenance are performed automatically. When the body is healthy, we don't have to consciously do anything about the secretion of our glands, the reproduction of our cells, the flow of current through the nerve circuits, and all the other autonomous functions. Other aspects, of course, depend on our conscious attention.

The aim of all body care and maintenance, even beyond the smooth running of the body, is the attainment of a state of physical well-being. In this state, verging on ecstasy, the body is in total physical contentment and thus transcends its own physicality. It exists in a state of 'I Am'. It has neither want nor need. It makes no demand on the consciousness, thus allowing consciousness to follow its own inclination to ascend.

To achieve this sense of physical well-being, your body must be at ease. Try this exercise: sit in a comfortable chair. Get the feel of how the chair is supporting you. Now, starting with your head, check out each part of your body for tensions, aches, or other forms the body's messages may take. Turn your head slowly from side to side, looking back over your shoulders. After turning it a few times, rest your head on your neck and shoulders in such a way that you don't have to carry it consciously.

When your head is balanced, take a deep breath and let it out. Now check your shoulders. Are they just hanging freely? Are your neck and shoulder muscles loose, resting easily on the frame of your body as it rests on the frame of your chair? (If you can't find a chair that is truly comfortable and suitable for this purpose, it is better to stand.)

Now ask yourself, "Are my shoulders resting on my spine? Is my spine resting on my pelvis?" And if you are sitting, "Is my pelvis resting on my buttocks, and is the chair carrying the whole thing so I don't have to do anything?" Work at this until the answer to all the questions is yes.

Exhale deeply and ask yourself, "What stands between me and total physical well-being? Is my body humming with ecstasy, or is it informing me that there are still things to be taken care of?" It's important to remember that you are not looking for ideas. Remind yourself, "I am scanning that me which is my body for a signal—its most current message on my state of being."

Few of us reach an ecstatic sense of well-being on our first try, so don't worry if you're feeling something less than ecstasy at this moment. Just take a deep breath and repeat the process. Ask yourself, "What stands in the way between where I am now and the place where I'd feel that sense of well-being?"

Probably several answers will quickly come to you (eat better; get more exercise; lose weight). Don't seize on them, because in all likelihood they come from a pre-programmed and inappropriate place that will lead you away from the present moment. Go back to your body and let the answer well up from it: "What stands between me and well-being at this very moment?"

The answer has nothing to do with what you ought to do or what you need to do (responsibilities and obligations). It has only to do with what your body is feeling right now.

The message from your body will consist of a feeling which may or may not be translatable into words. If words do form, there will be only one or two. They are important words; try to remember them.

Next, ask yourself how to acknowledge the body's message. What has to be done about the words or feeling, so that your body will know you've gotten the message and that you intend to do something about it? What step is necessary to move from the place and condition in which you now are, past the obstacles indicated by your own body, to a place of well-being?

Wait for the answer. When it comes, it too will be a body

sense, but it will concern something that can be done *now* (like, relax the muscles in your forehead; take off your shoes; release the tension in your calves).

When you have done this, check with your body once again. Has the action you've just performed taken care of the immediate problem? Is your body at ease, is it sighing? ("A sigh breaks one's body," said Reb Moshe Leib.) Or is there still something else in the way?

If there is, repeat the procedure. Repeat it until your body is content, until every fiber and cell begins to hum. Repeat the process until your body is clarified and lucid, so transparent it seems to have disappeared.

When you have reached this state, you've given your body to God and your soul is sure to follow.

JEWISH
ORIENTATION

The word orientation originally meant to turn toward the Orient, toward the rising sun. It has come to mean the process by which we establish where we stand in relationship to everything else. It's what we do when we want to get our bearings.

Two forms of orientation are of interest to us here: one in which we seek to get in step with the processes of the universe, and another in which we align ourselves with our cumulative past.

GOD IS THE VERB ENERGIZING
THE UNIVERSE

In the realm of spiritual matters, the Bible enjoins us to orient ourselves toward the Holy Land when we pray. This is why the Holy Ark, which houses the Torah, is always placed on the eastern wall of the synagogue, toward the Holy Land—when you face the Ark, you automatically face the Holy Land and are in a Jewish orientation for prayer. Since we live to the west of Israel, we turn to the east; whenever we participate in a sunrise service, we achieve the same effect.

This level of orientation is physical and geographical. It is one of the levels of orientation which are available to us, but many people minimize it and think of it only as geography. However, the same passage in the Bible telling us to orient ourselves geographically (Kings I, 8:48) also enjoins us to turn toward God with all our heart and all our soul. This more complicated process requires greater energy.

For this orientation, we go beneath the surface into the endlessly rich inner world of the self. Here we deal with the intentions and secrets of our own hearts, with our desires, goals, and energies, and line them up with God.

The God I'm talking about is neither the Old Man with the flowing white beard nor the Great Mother giving birth to the universe, though these images do have their place. In this instance, I mean God as the Verb energizing the universe, God as the Source of all movement.

The energy flows everywhere; it is how God "gods." It flows in cycles, in waves, in constant lines of force, in every metaphor and simile we can imagine. We can't control this energy; all we can do is recognize it and get in step with it, in sync, so that our very existence is in harmony with what is rather than at cross-purposes with it. This is the great orientation; it puts us in phase with the rest of creation. When we orient ourselves toward the multitudinous and diverse creatures of the world, we face the verse (the many in a combined form) of the universe. And when we turn toward the One, we face the uni of the universe. The tide flows into the many and ebbs into the One.

Once we orient with the flow of God energy, and bring ourselves to the point where we consciously and inten-

tionally exist in harmony with it, we too become ener-
gizers. Instead of impeding the flow of the universe,
which we do when we're out of alignment, we reinforce it.

In the practical terms of our daily lives, being in harmony with the universe entails a commitment to such
endeavours as conservation, preservation, ecological concern, organicity, and appropriateness. These concerns
have always been central to the Jewish view of life and
code of behavior. Indeed, the whole issue of kosher can be
viewed as an attempt to provide a guide to appropriate
behavior. Thus we can be either kosher (appropriately
ready and prepared, in harmony with God's call) or treif
(torn from the Divine milieu).

WHAT IS KOSHER?

Sometimes I think we Jews exist so that in every age we
will be able to ask our eternal question: Is it kosher?
Kosher means clean, pure and, by extension, good for the
natural processes of the universe. The opposite of kosher
is treif, which means unclean, impure, polluted, and
hence polluting. Kosher is energy-efficient and productive; treif is wasteful and eventually destructive.

Taken in its narrow sense, keeping kosher is seen as a
matter of obedience and submission to the Law. In this
view, the Law is approached as statutes decreed by human
beings. But the laws of religion, like the laws of nature, are
integral elements of the cosmos. The law of gravity, for
example, was not legislated; it was discovered. It was
discovered because it exists, because it is natural. And so,
too, the laws of religion—which are God's message to us
on how to live in harmony with the rest of creation—were
revealed/discovered to be embedded in existence.

In the past, many people were attracted to religion by burning bushes, supernatural occurrences introduced into their routine lives. Extraordinary miracles proclaimed religions and legitimized them. Today, when I talk about religion, I stress the miracle of the obvious. God reveals and creates constantly in the ordinary. There we find the real expression of His Minding.

DOES GOD MIND?

In an age of increasingly rapid technological change, the issue of what's kosher has widened its focus to an inclusive concern for the well-being of all our fellow human beings, our planet, and the entire universe. As soon as we orient ourselves to the path of planetary survival, we must ask about a whole range of things: are they kosher?

We want to know if nuclear power is kosher, and the electricity produced by it. (And what about nuclear waste, and all the other toxins with which we pollute the air, the earth, the seas, and eventually ourselves—are they clean or unclean, kosher or treif?)

Eggs are generally considered kosher, but what about eggs from chickens who spend their entire lives imprisoned in a cage one cubic foot in size? Food pellets are brought to them on one conveyor belt; their droppings and eggs are taken away on another. The Bible forbids us to torment animals or cause them any unnecessary grief. Raising chickens who can go out sometimes and see the sky or eat a worm or blade of grass is one thing, but manufacturing them in the concentration camp conditions of contemporary "poultry ranches" is quite another.

According to Jewish dietary laws, all fruits and vegetables are *kosher*. But what about green beans or tomatoes harvested by ill-treated, underpaid, and exploited migrant workers—are they *kosher*? What about bananas from countries ruled by despots where the workers have few rights, and the bananas are heavily sprayed with DDT, picked green, and then artificially ripened in the holds of ships by being gassed—are they *kosher*?

Are chemical food additives *kosher*? They give food a longer shelf life, but what do they do to our lives? Who really knows what all those chemicals do to our livers, kidneys, stomachs, or intestines? And artificial coloring dyes which make food look "pretty" but may cause cancer—are they *kosher*? And cigarettes, which we already *know* cause cancer, heart disease, and other health problems—are they *kosher* and pure?

The list of things about which we must answer the question—is it *kosher*?—is endless: fur from baby seals clubbed to death? Products from endangered species? The chemicals contained in many prepared foods (look at the list of ingredients on some labels)? Products or services produced at the cost of human pain and misery? Coal from strip mines which destroy the land; oil from offshore wells which pollute the seas? After a moment's thought, you can easily add to this list.

As you can see, the concept of *kosher* has to do with both the individual and the universe. Helping to take care of the business of the universe begins with taking care of ourselves. The Jewish tradition is very clear about this. Each of us is part of the whole and we matter. We are therefore obliged to treat the temples of our bodies with the respect, gratitude, and even awe they deserve.

Once we have learned to care for ourselves—as individuals, as families, as groups, as an entire species of human beings—we reestablish our organic connection with the will of God. This organic connection is neither abstract nor supernatural. It is based on a functional response to the ongoing processes of the universe. To discover these processes, all we have to do is open our hearts and eyes. If there is any great heresy, it is in making ourselves opaque to the world.

A HUNDRED GENERATIONS OF ANCESTORS

Many of us are looking for roots today, feeling disconnected from our traditions by the fragmentation of contemporary life. We've lost our sense of being legitimate members of the universe; we feel like strangers passing through someone else's territory. But this disorientation is not a necessary feature of modern life. There are ways to anchor ourselves, ways to regain a sense of belonging. One, which we've just discussed, calls for getting in step with the processes of the universe. Another is to reacquaint ourselves with our ancestral legacies.

It is important to know where we're coming from in order to understand where we are, and perhaps even where we are going. This requires a look backward into the past of our ancestors. The exploration is not without risk—there is always the danger of being trapped and tyrannized by the past. People sometimes slip into the assumption that whatever was done back then was the *real* thing; if it was good enough for them, it's good enough for us; give me that old time religion! These are the sentiments of the fundamentalists, but they are not the sentiments we are talking about here.

When we look back at our ancestors, our aim is not to be locked into the past. We want to use the past as a reference point, a source of tradition, and a living history so that we will be able to see ourselves as links in a long chain of continuity.

If we open ourselves to the potential impact of our ancestors and allow ourselves to be influenced by the accumulated experience of the Jewish past, we begin to tap a great source of energy. This energy, in one form or another, is readily available, but many people ignore it or pretend it doesn't exist.

To get in touch with it, we must project ourselves into the experience or frame of mind of our ancestors. This is easier than it sounds, for in practice what we have to do is follow certain procedures or perform certain acts in the style our ancestors have used for thousands of years. When we do this (and let's say we go back around 3000 years to the time of Moses), we contact and in some way resurrect at least one hundred generations of ancestors behind us and within us.

A hundred generations represents an immense mountain of human experience; the encounter creates a very real impact. If you view your ancestors as a pyramid—two parents, four grandparents, eight great-grandparents, sixteen great-great-grandparents, 2048 great-great-great-great-great-great-great-great-great grandparents (eleven generations)—and if you tap the energy concentrated at the tip of the pyramid, which is your location, you can begin to make use of your birthright.

It's the anniversary of your grandfather's death, the *Yahrzeit*, when tradition requires the lighting of a twenty-four-hour candle and the recitation of the mourner's prayer for the dead. Sometimes you have a strong sense of your grandfather's presence, but usually this feeling occurs spontaneously, or is evoked by an accidental, unplanned chain of associations. This day, however, when

you feel a special need to be in touch with your grandfather, he is not very present. So you make a conscious
effort.

You think about him, try to remember what his voice
sounded like, or the aroma of his body when he hugged
you, or some other intensely personal feature. Then you
look around for a memento, an object your grandfather
used—a winecup, penknife, prayer book, watch fob. You
pick up the object, handle it, and in some way which you
cannot entirely understand, a connection is made. Perhaps the physical object jogs your memories. Perhaps
something of your grandfather has been absorbed by the
object.

But whatever the cause, the experience remains. Once
again, you feel close to him, and perhaps you also feel
some sadness that he is no longer alive. But beyond your
grandfather, in fact *by way of* him, you also feel connected
to the pyramid of all your ancestors in a very conscious
way. You feel rooted and grounded, and full of an energy
and strength that comes from a sense of continuity and
belonging. Your grandfather was the source of one quarter
of your *you*, your *being*, so the grandfather within you
always has the power to energize you.

The search for roots is a perfect metaphor for what
people want. Roots connect us with our environment and
absorb nourishment from it. In their quest to reconnect
with their roots and find their legitimate places in the
universe, many people open themselves to experiences
and rituals from which their ancestors derived meaning
and ecstasy. For Jews, one of the strongest of these stimuli
is the sound of the *shofar*, the hollow ram's horn that is
blown on certain holy occasions.

When a Jew hears the call of the *shofar*, it is a rich,
many-layered experience encompassing a wide range of
feelings. When we are in earshot, this ancient sound

pierces our thoughts, our feelings, the very core of our being. It raises goose bumps on our souls. This is because we hear it with our own ears and also with the ears of our great-grandparents and great-great-grandparents.

At times like this, when we touch a live wire of tradition, something mysterious takes place, something we cannot name or rationally assess. These experiences are the kinds of phenomena that Jung and many anthropologists have talked about, though they too have had no explanation. The moments remain mysterious, but their authenticity is undiminished.

Judaism seldom lets us do anything important when we are less than totally awake. When we are alert to the presence of the unknown, what results is often a sharp rise in the level of our consciousness.

To take a powerful example, we don't know exactly what happens at the moment of circumcision. (See "How to Deal With a Jewish Issue: Circumcision"), but the experience involves both the personal and the historical—the specific parents and child on the one hand, and the chain of Jewish ancestors on the other, a chain stretching all the way back to Abraham. The parents who present their son for circumcision enter a special space. At the moment of circumcision, it's as if they are holding their son in their laps, and their parents are holding them, and they in turn are being held by their parents, and so on for a hundred generations.

Many people are cut off from the power in the pyramid of ancestors because they don't believe in it. Their consciousness is active only in the physical world; they have allowed themselves to become blind to the nonphysical, spiritual world. The problem is that the physical world cannot provide everything we need to be healthy, fully-developed beings. There are essential vitamins that are not to be found there. Most of us are starved for these spiritual nourishments, whether we know it or not. The sad irony is that these vitamins are not scarce but available, if only the people who are hungry for them knew where to look. All they need is an eye-opener, which may take various forms.

One Sunday morning, as I was preparing to leave a Sabbath weekend retreat and head home, a man came over to me and said, "I want to thank you. Something incredible happened to me this weekend. I learned how to pray."

I was in a hurry, but for this I had time. So I sat down and listened. He'd never been on a retreat before, nor had he ever participated publicly in a religious activity which called on him to be conscious of his true feelings. His breakthrough had come on Friday night, when we had formed a prayer circle after lighting the Sabbath candles.

"I was standing there in the circle," he said, "trying to focus my mind. I had been feeling bored and lonely earlier, and now I felt a little foolish, holding hands with a bunch of strangers and trying to think a holy thought.

"I realized that I was drooping over and began to straighten my spine, but at that moment something started happening inside of me. And I wasn't self-conscious, which surprised me. Like the other people in the circle, I didn't care any more how I looked. I gave in to this new feeling. All that mattered was what was happening to me.

"It was like a bubble rising inside of me and it choked me to tears. Not because I was depressed or had a reason to cry. What was coming up in me felt like, Oooo, it's been wanting to come out for such a long, long time and hasn't had a chance, and now here it is, in this setting and with the support of all these people. And I saw the faces of everybody shining and the Sabbath candles reflected in their eyes. And I felt, although I had never met any of these people before, that I was certainly at home."

One evening at a coffee hour after a lecture, a woman told a story. She hadn't had much active contact with Judaism for a long time, but she'd come to hear my talk because of something that had happened to her a few weeks earlier, and she wanted to know if I could give her advice.

"Several weeks ago I was out shopping when a bearded man dressed in black approached me on the sidewalk and asked if I was Jewish. He seemed to come from some Hasidic group. They had a van parked at the curb, and there were several of these men there.

"When I told him I was Jewish, he gave me a pair of small candlesticks made of stamped out metal and asked me to light candles on Friday evening. He even gave me the candles, told me what time to do it, and handed me a card with the words of a prayer written in phonetic English.

"At home I put the candlesticks on the table and forgot about them for a day or two. But on Friday afternoon when I got home, they were the first thing that caught my eye. I looked at them. They were very simple and plain, nothing like the candlesticks I use for a candlelight dinner, but there was something about them that attracted me.

"I remembered going to my grandmother's house sometimes on Friday afternoons, and how she'd have her candles on the table too. So I looked at the clock, and about the time the man said to do it, I lit the candles and said the words on the card.

"I want to tell you this. I don't understand why and

how, but something happened. I was quiet for awhile. I kept on looking at the candles. I even remembered how my grandmother used to make this motion—round circles through the air with her hands, as if to bring the light close to herself, and then cover her face. I did that too.

"And I started to cry. I don't know why. It was bittersweet. I felt in touch with things in my life I'd given up on, things which turned out to have a lot of meaning for me. At the same time another voice from inside was telling me I was being sentimental and silly over a pair of cheap little candlesticks. But I'd had that feeling, like seeing a very dear friend after a long separation, and I wanted to feel it again.

"I've been trying to do it since. Somehow, I think there's more to it than just saying those words and making those motions with your hands. What should I do?"

I smiled at her and praised God. She had already begun to do what she had to do to reinforce her connection with what she called *that feeling*. The best light from the Sabbath candles is not the light on the outside, it's the light within us; and her inner light had been rekindled. Now it was like a beacon, orienting her to the riches of her birthright.

PRAYER—
FACT OR FEELING?

Too frequently, we analyze and hold forth as if the religious experience had to do only with information. If information were the key ingredient, we could feed the data into a computer, program the computer for prayer, and never have to think about it again.

But that is not the reality. Explications of religions have their place; histories, philosophies, and sociologies of religions also have their place. But they do not and cannot replace the *religious experience itself*.

As for Judaism, I believe it has gone a long way toward becoming an elite religion: highly prescriptive, oververbalized and intellectualized, and underexperienced. In order to overcome these trends, I introduce people to the experiences in Jewish ritual and observance, sensitizing them to the psychological and emotional content rather than the outer form. People then realize that religious acts are natural unfoldings of our response to God's call. When they learn how to recreate these acts, they move naturally closer and closer to the intent of the ritual. They become aware that the ritual is the soul's way of dancing with God.

Let me give you several different examples to make this

83

point clear. First, let us look at the blessings, or the *brakhot.*

Tradition expects a person to recite the blessings which the Rabbis prescribed. According to the law, everything of the world belongs to God—"the earth is the Lord's and the fullness thereof." And yet, "He has given the earth to human beings." A blessing is a means of acquiring something of the God-given world. And it works when it is more than a legal move, when it is the response of a heart.

If a person wants to learn how to say the blessings and what they are really about, I say: "Every time you feel something good happening to you or even something tough or painful say: 'Blessed are you, Lord our God, (*Barukh attah Adonai*), you make the sun shine. Blessed are you, Lord our God . . . today is a beautiful day. Blessed are you, Lord our God . . . the air is so polluted it is amazing that I am still alive.'" Each time a person focuses in this way, blessings become a reality, and the person begins to learn about prayer and life.

In a similar vein, when a person asks me how to start praying (*davening*), I suggest not using the prayer book (*siddur*) for a while. First, recognize the chain that connects you to God through your ancestors. Make a blessing (*brakhah*) and thank God for that. Then recognize the chain that connects you to life and make a blessing for that. Then recognize the chain that connects you with holiness. Now, begin asking for the things you need.

The first thing you need is the good sense to know what to ask for. Ask for *sekhel*, common sense.

At this point you might wonder, "Who am I to ask anything of God?" If you ask this because you feel so far away from God, pray to get closer.

If you begin to recall things you've done which you consider wrong, pray for forgiveness.

Pray for help in the struggle to live. Pray for emotional or physical healing. Pray to make a decent living.

As your prayer unfolds, you'll recognize its natural, human content. It's flowing out of you. When you make a request and seal it with, "Thank you, God," you close the circle and get closer to the inner content of the prayer.

THE PRAYER BOOK

When you pray from a *siddur* (prayer book), you'll see that such a prayer already exists—the *Sh'moneh Essray.* The *siddur,* then, can be a guide to replicating the process you began on your own.

In most Jewish circles today, the use of the *siddur* has come to be highly misunderstood. The problem goes back to the nineteenth century and its overemphasis on rationality. Many Jews in the nineteenth century saw the *siddur* as a book of information. This misconception remains widespread today, as when, for example, the prayer book specifies that a passage be said three times and many people disregard the instruction. For information, one time is enough. But the prayer book is a guide for offering the heart's feelings to God. To understand how that is possible, you have to see the *siddur* in an entirely different way.

When I am out of touch with the purpose of the prayer book, I settle down in the synagogue and my body goes into the posture it would assume if I were about to read a text for information. I look in the front of the book to find out what committee worked on it. I look in the back to see who the contributors were. Very quickly I become bored; I do not know what to do with it anymore.

The whole experience changes if I sit with a kind of

body eagerness. I hold the *siddur* in my left hand, scanning the line to be recited. I do not pray into the *siddur*. I pick a phrase, look away from the book, focus toward the Presence of God and repeat it. When I look in the *siddur* I do not recite; when I recite the phrase, I visualize the content of the words and I do not look in. I project my voice to get into the feeling of the phrase. I breathe in a way conducive to the rhythm of my recital. I *shuckle* (sway back and forth, bend my knees) with my body, make gestures and both create and acknowledge the feeling that results.

In this way, I can say the same stuff I said last week again. It is like a husband saying to his wife, "I love you." What is he talking about? He is not giving her new information. If she sees it as information, she says, "Stop. You told me already—enough!" But he says, "I am not telling you this for information. I have a feeling and this is the best way I can express it: 'Dear, I love you!'" *Davening* and the *siddur* are vehicles for expressing those feelings, and not for information. How many times can you say: "I love you?" As many times as you have the feeling and energy to put into it.

Even the prayer language chosen by those of the nineteenth century reflects their bias against feeling-words. "Sanctuary" is for the head; "holy place" is for the heart. I encourage you to make your own paraphrases of texts, in a language you understand and to which you can relate. A faithful translation of what the Hebrew says, in words from your own time and place, allows the process to have real significance.

PRAYING IN
GOD'S CORNER

Iff you talk to God, you're religious; if He answers, you're psychotic." Such is the inconsistent view of the rationalist. In this wry sentence, the psychiatrist Thomas S. Szasz neatly sums up the ironic dilemma of trying to understand the *spiritual* by approaching it on the level of the intellect. Such an effort may provide philosophical entertainment, but it does not get you any closer to God, or help your conversation with Him. You can take so long analyzing your relationship to God that you never get around to the *experience*; you can spend too much time talking *about* Him and not enough talking *to* Him.

When approaching God, it is best to turn down your mental computer and switch over to your feelings, even if this makes you self-conscious or appear foolish in your own eyes. For talking to God, the intellect is not the best tool; God is not interested in your I.Q., nor is He impressed by your learning. The heartfelt prayers of an unlearned person are worth more than the perfunctory recitations of the scholar.

We meet God in time and space. In one sense, we enter His spatial aspect when we place ourselves in His presence. Abraham Joshua Heschel wrote: "We cannot make God visible to us, but we can make ourselves visible to Him."

A specific setting or atmosphere is not required when you want to place yourself in God's presence, but obviously some settings are more conducive to prayer than others. Watching a sunrise on a mountain top is usually a helpful place; a crowded subway car at rush hour is more difficult. It is a fact, though, that sometimes we fail to make contact in the most appropriate settings and succeed in those that would seem to be most dismal.

Still, we need all the help we can get. Generally speaking, there is a proper time and place for everything. This old saying is the underlying message of Ecclesiastes, and it is one of the great truths: the universe unfolds in an endless sequence of appropriate actions and reactions. In its broadest meaning, this concept deals with the workings of the physical universe of galaxies and solar systems, of electrons and neutrons. In a more finite, human sense, it suggests that something that is right for one time and place is wrong for another; that something difficult or impossible in one time or place may flow freely in another.

Most of us set aside special places at home for specific activities—a reading chair, a sewing corner, a hobby table. The reason is clear; a space intentionally planned for a specific activity will enhance the performance of that activity. Similarly, it helps to set aside a place to pray, a place to talk with God.

God's corner does not have to be elaborate; probably, the simpler it is, the better. It should, however, be a place in which you can totally relax and feel comfortable. God is already there: create an atmosphere to help you talk with Him. Light candles; candlelight is richer than electric light. Set your senses free of their ordinary, everyday fare. In this way, they will respond freshly rather than by habit. Some incense or other aromatic substance may help lead your senses away from the mundane and toward the spiritual. You also might want to have a pad of paper and a pencil handy, in the event that you want to jot down an insight.

When the physical space of God's corner is prepared, consider the element of time. When should you use that space and how frequently?

First of all, some form of regularity is important. Scheduled expectations have a way of fulfilling themselves. So it is a good idea to establish a regular timetable. Prayer times are best established by the rhythm of the day and our own internal rhythms. For the purposes of prayer, we want to be in touch with the *cyclical time* of a day's actual coming and going rather than with the *linear time* ticked away second by second on the clock.

Universal traditions, including the 'traditions' of the animals, point to dawn and dusk as the most fitting times to reach out beyond ourselves. They are in-between times, rich and suggestive times when light and darkness blend together, when two contrary qualities coexist in the same time and space—the best times for prayer.

"He makes the day to pass and brings on the night." In our hearts we know the night will pass and day will come again. God is manifested in cyclical time, in the recurring flow of recreation. Words of praise and thanks then come easily to our consciousness: "Oh, ever living and existing God, may You always rule over us."

In the Jewish tradition, two periods of time are held to be especially good for sitting in God's presence. One is the period during which the sunlight fades away at dusk, and the other is the period between the rising of the morning star and the appearance of the first rays of the sun. At such times your whole being will respond, in agreement with the natural cycle.

After you have created an atmosphere and found a time, lie back on pillows or assume a position that allows your physical self to be as comfortable as possible. Focus on your body, using some of the techniques suggested in "The Teachings of the Body." Breathe deeply, in and out. Relax your muscles, one by one, until they are as tension-less as possible. Exhale with a sigh, as heartfelt as you can allow yourself, and begin to talk.

Don't worry if you have no words ready. The words will come. Most likely you will feel foolish saying words to the candles when there is no one in sight. Don't get caught up in this feeling. Dismiss it. It is appropriate to your relationship with other human beings but inappropriate with God. So begin to talk, and get the words out of your mouth in as pure a form as you can, without dressing them up, or editing, or hedging.

It might occur to you that you are only going through some empty motions, since God by His very nature knows everything. In His omnipotence, God already does know, but that is not the point. The value you get from talking to God is in the conscious, intentional act of presenting yourself—thoughts, feelings, and all. It is standing naked before God, opening your heart to Him, to Her, and saying with every cell and tissue and glimmer of awareness in your being, "HERE I AM! THIS IS ME. THIS IS HOW I AM."

It's natural to experience a buzz of digressions and self-consciousness. Bear with it. It might last a while, but it will pass. Then something else will happen.

From a deep place in your heart, an affirmation will rise that what you are doing now is the right thing to be doing. You will try to speak. Perhaps you'll say a word or two. Before you know it, you'll be crying. Tears will stream down your face, not bitter tears of grief, not tears of anguish or rage, but tears from your heart, sweet tears. These tears are the prayers of your soul, prayers for which you have not yet found the right words.

Don't be frightened when you start to cry. It's all right. You've placed yourself in a highly charged situation. It is no small thing to consciously present yourself to God and bare your heart. Some people say it's like taking hold of a live wire. Others say it's like stepping off a cliff and not falling. Tears are a very common response. Most people who have had spiritual experiences in the presence of God are familiar with them.*

At first, when the soul is mute and untutored, you won't have the words to express the deep feelings that rise to your own awareness at the moment you want to present them to God. Nevertheless, you will try. You will speak falteringly, perhaps with great effort. But you will speak.

The words will begin to come; you'll hear them with your own ears. Let the flow continue. Keep the process going. Tell God what you feel in the most private part of your being. Keep aiming for the raw, unadorned truth.

You don't have to impress God; He is not impressible. There is no competition involved, nor any other game. You will say things to Him that you've never been able to say to anyone, including yourself. At times, your ears will hear words from your own mouth that will shock and pain you. But don't stop.

As the process of peeling away the layers of yourself continues, keep talking. Present the process to God, step by step. Say everything. Say whatever wells up, and as soon as you understand that there is another layer of truth beneath it, tell God. Say something like "God, I still have

---

*Tears are infinitely expressive. At an early period of his life, the Baal Shem Tov (called the Besht) worked as a *shochet*, one who slaughters animals in the manner prescribed by Jewish Law. The rule is to cause as little pain as possible, so the knife must be honed to perfection. When the Besht sharpened his knife, he wet the sharpening stone with his tears.

to give you a deeper truth of me." Then say the next layer
as it rises up in you.

When you have gotten this far, you have accomplished
much. The process is in motion. You are truly talking to
God. Now it is His turn to talk to you.

Every once in a while, pause, sit back, breathe deeply.
Become passive and allow for a response. Invite a reply to
form in your consciousness. If particularly strong
thoughts occur to you at this moment, you may want to
write them down.

Instead of or in addition to this passive approach, you
might even offer your mouth as an instrument of divine
reply. On this matter, the Baal Shem Tov once said, "When
I weld my spirit to God, I let my mouth say what it will,
for then all my words are bound to their root in Heaven."
Perhaps you will say words or even phrases, or receive
indications on the inner plane in silence. In whatever
form they take, these words or indications are God's reply
to you and your needs.

At this moment, you will probably experience a sweet
feeling in your entire being. Relish it. Enjoy it. It is from
God. It is a manifestation of God in you, and you deserve
it.

You have just communicated with the cosmos, an act of
the greatest moment because it is a conscious recognition
of the living universe. Further, it is your intentional attempt to get in tune with the universe. The content of your
message—whatever you are experiencing at the moment—
is not what matters most. The key is the act itself, the
recognition that the universe is alive and responsive in
you and to you.

Talking to God once can be an electrifying experience.
Talking to Him regularly will nourish your soul and
change your life.

SINGING TO GOD

Once at a week-long conference and workshop on higher spirituality, I led a group of people in a ritual which called for parading around the room in a circle while we invited the stars, the trees, the clouds, the birds, and all the other natural beings to sing praises to God. At first there was some tentativeness, some self-consciousness, but by the time we got to the clouds, everyone was singing. As it usually does, this exercise released a great deal of energy. Before it was over, all of us were not only singing, we were singing with joy and delight.

After the workshop, a man came up to me and said, "Something happened to me once when I was a boy in music class. We were singing and the teacher walked by and listened to me. She made a sour face; then she leaned over and whispered, 'You just move your lips. You'll be a silent one.' And since that day, I have never sung. That was thirty-five years ago. Today was the first time I sang since then. When we began singing the hallelujahs and everybody joined in, I found myself opening up. I was singing before I knew it. All of a sudden, I found that I could."

As I listened to this man, I knew he was talking not only about singing with his mouth, but about soul singing. He was talking of worship and ecstasy, the healing glow you feel when you are in harmony with the universe.

It happened for him at the moment we were chanting the great hallelujahs together, making harmony toward each other and toward the universe in a loving way.

It happened when we sang of how we are like kings and queens of the earth, and judges and trees and sea monsters and fire and hail and snow, and old folks and little kids, and young men and maidens. And with each hallelujah, he flew.

It certainly had something to do with singing, but singing was only the body of it. On top of the body of the song was the spirit of the song. And because the setting was right and the people were supportive of each other, and because the singer welcomed it, the spirit grew wings and took his soul for a ride.

He needed to sing and he needed to fly while he was singing. He needed to feel perfectly free to sing with as much unrestrained joy as he could muster. He also needed to feel entitled and worthy of singing. Everybody has these needs, but many people never have them fulfilled because they have been frightened off. In their earliest experiences with song, they were made to fear that somebody was watching and correcting them. They were fed the notion that they had to perform, to please somebody else. The truth, however, is very different. The basic origin of song is the sigh, either of pain or of joy. "I am so happy I could sing all day" means just that. We don't have to please anyone with our singing. We can just allow what is bubbling up in our hearts to flow forth freely in song and rejoice in it.

What this man needed, as so many other people do, was to rediscover the connection between his performance and his feelings; between singing out and elation. But he had been denied that because of what the unthinking teacher had, in effect, said to him: "Your exuberance and enthusiasm are very nice, but you sing off-key. Your performance is lousy." Since that time, his performance had been cut off, his enthusiasm had no way to express itself, and the flow of his feelings was blocked.

On this occasion, he got what he needed by seeing other people let go and drop their own fears about performing poorly, the very thing he could not allow himself to do. As we paraded around in our circle, singing hallelujah, playing the roles of trees and sea monsters and fire and hail and creeping things and winged fowl, he opened up. By finding that there were other people in the same situation who were willing to let go, he found the courage to let go too. In doing so, *the man gave himself permission*. He needed help, but ultimately only he could do it.

Though he'd been denied permission to sing in the school choir, which had to be perfect and harmonious, he did have permission to sing in this choir, which was spontaneous, without any requirements other than desire, and which was received by God on the wings of *intention*.

The man had a religious experience, as we all did. Perhaps the experience did not conform to a preconceived format or ritual, but its content was genuine. It was heartfelt and holy. I am not at all sure that the symbols and forms usually associated with the word *religion* are as crucial as the experience itself. A well-functioning religious person, in my view, is one who uses the symbols and tools of his religion as means to generate genuine experiences in which there is a heightened awareness of the universe and a closer connection to God.

Sometimes, as we've seen, we are prevented from having these vital, necessary experiences by the actions of others. Often the incidents which undermine our self-esteem and suppress our ability for self-expression are unintentional. In all likelihood, the teacher who hadn't liked his voice had no idea her harsh criticism would affect this man's life so deeply. Without a thought, she cut him off from song.

That was a very great loss. From the Hasidic point of view, songs of joy open the gates of Heaven. This joy is in the heart of the singer, not in the ear of the listener. Just as all songs are beautiful to Him, so too are all rituals which follow and respond to the processes of His universe. All forms of prayer are pleasing to God, so long as their aim is to know Him in all His ways.

When it comes right down to it, we must give ourselves permission to sing, in all the multiple meanings of that word. We are the only ones who can do it. Such permission-giving is an aspect of taking our lives seriously, and accepting our roles as meaningful, vital parts of the universe.

On another level, there is an even greater responsibility. In moments of deep meditation, we sometimes see in a flash of insight that we are not only parts of the universe, but that *we are it*. In those blinding moments, we feel that our songs are the only things that hold it all together and bring us into harmony with God.

It is our natural function to reciprocate God's love by keeping the organic energy of the universe flowing any way we can.

Improvisation and spontaneity are powerful virtues. Once the Baal Shem Tov was praying on Yom Kippur with a group of Hasidim. Normally, the Besht's prayers rose to Heaven like flocks of birds, but on this day everything seemed constrained. It was as if the souls of all those present were held down by chains of doubt, like the man who could not sing.

Despite great efforts, no prayers took flight. The Besht strained, hoping to break through and make contact, to reach an at-one-ment. But nothing happened.

In the group was a father and his young son. The father was an upright man, but the son had shown little interest in prayer or other traditional forms. He usually spent his time watching his father's small flock on the hills and meadows. While he watched over them, it was his habit to play on a small whistle, which he always carried in his pocket.

As the tension mounted in the shul, all eyes on the Besht at his prayer, the boy got caught up in the effort and wanted to help. Instinctively, he reached for his whistle. His father tried to stop him, but the boy pulled the whistle out of his pocket, brought it to his lips, and blew a piercing note. TWEET!

The father was deeply embarrassed. Everyone turned to the boy with scowls on their faces. Everyone except the Besht, for at that moment the chains which had shackled prayer were suddenly snapped. Free of restraint, the Besht's prayers rose up like swallows and flew straight to God. The Besht turned to the people, his face radiant with joy, and said, "Don't reprimand the boy. It was the song of his whistle that carried our prayer up to Heaven."

Nobody had ever heard of blowing a whistle during the Yom Kippur prayer, but the boy did it and the Besht approved. It was appropriate because it was a pure offering. In a completely natural, unselfconscious way, the boy offered up his best intentions. He released his song like a bird, without a thought about permission, and the song was sweet to God.

HOW TO DEAL
WITH A JEWISH ISSUE:
CIRCUMCISION

You have been involved in a natural birth and are now the parents of a baby son. You did it at home, or in surroundings that resembled a home setting as much as possible. You incorporated everything that has to do with gentleness and tried to avoid all violence. Now as your son is about to become eight days old, you have to make a decision. Will he be circumcised or not? And if the answer is yes, will there be a traditional *Bris* (ritual Jewish circumcision) or not? You wish you did not have to take your baby, a new person who loves and trusts you, and inflict the trauma of an operation on him. Yes, *inflict* is the word, let's not make it pretty.

You have already been through some of the literature and have weighed the possible medical advantages which might accrue as a result: reduced probability of cervical or uterine cancer in your son's future mate; the hygienic benefits to the child himself; and so on. But it does not add up, and you are in conflict.

Parents, relatives, and friends are exerting pressure with their expectations of a *Bris*, and you yourself would also love to have a celebration for family rejoicing, if only you did not have to do it in this form. You associate circumcision with barbaric customs practiced by uncivilized people, and you wish you didn't have to participate in such a brutal procedure.

At a deeper level there are other conflicts. You espoused and followed natural methods for the birth. You believe perfection lies in following the natural flow. Had God-Nature wanted boys to be without prepuces, they would be born that way. But your hesitation about your own son is balanced by your expectations of others: if the child were somebody else's, you would probably expect him to be circumcised. You find that your objections to circumcision are not absolute.

You are experiencing the pain and discomfort for your child in anticipation of his pain, the same way parents always have, telling their children, "It hurts me more than it hurts you." The anticipation is yours only; the baby is not caught in the anxiety because he does not know what is in the offing. You do, and this nagging discomfort makes you want to be past the experience.

Conversations with other parents confirm your feelings: they too felt as you do before the *Bris*. And so it has always been, and must be—that the mother and father sense a tightening in themselves up to the moment and even a little while after. It is a difficult, gut-wrenching experience, and all Jewish parents of a son must face it because it's an unavoidable feature of the Jewish landscape. Usually the decision is yes, but it's not arrived at without soul searching, hesitation, questions, or anguish. When it's over, though, it almost always turns out that it wasn't so bad after all.

After the *Bris*, one father said, "I felt I was being asked if I would allow *myself* to be circumcised, as I am now, as an adult. Shivers ran through me at the thought of the pain. But when I remembered the labor pains my wife endured when our son was born, I felt ashamed. I answered yes to the question. I thought, yes, I want to."

"My child is not someone to do this to!" a mother said. "The feeling came right out of my guts. No one has a right do this to MY CHILD! Then I heard an echo . . .! '*Whose* child?' Do I own him or is he mine to care for until he is old enough to care for himself? Do I have the right to make a decision which might lead him *away* from his birthright, or is that a decision only he can make when he is old enough?

"While I was pregnant I felt the need to get in touch with my roots. I can go back only three generations on my father's side and fewer on my mother's. Then I gave birth and my son was here. I felt the roots extending all the way back to Abraham. It was a connection that came out of my body. It occurred to me that men could never experience labor and birth and the knowing that came with it. I *knew* that women have a secret that men cannot share. Maybe, I thought, the *Bris* is a secret for males which we cannot share. It was painful, but I felt I had to let go and allow my child to be initiated this way so he could belong to the world of Jewish men."

After the *Bris* of her son, another mother reported: "I had a lot of trouble letting this happen. As it turned out, I don't think it was really so bad on my baby. He's made worse faces with colic. Somehow I felt he was sealed into his body by the *Bris* and the pain. Before he was sort of in and out, not yet fully grounded. Since the *Bris*, he has become a person.

"There was another reason I decided on the *Bris*. All the men in my family have always been circumcised and I didn't want my son to be the first one who was not. Also, I didn't want my son to have a strange-looking penis. Somehow, my son's uncircumcised penis would make me think of him as an outsider. All my life I have wanted to have a big *Mishpoche* (family circle)—uncles, aunts, cousins. Some of my friends had, and I envied them. When all the people of our Havura, and relatives and other friends came and helped us celebrate, I felt my baby had connected with a *Mishpoche*."

Covenant is a large word in Judaism. We have made a contract with God. He will be our God and we will be His people. For Jewish men, the sign of this Covenant is circumcision. The word circumcision remains a medical term and confuses the issue; henceforth, we'll call it by its Hebrew name: *Milah* or *Bris Milah*.

Bris Milah is the seal, the sign of the Covenant. We are not the only ones who have this sign. Since it is a Covenant made with Abraham-Ibrahim, it is also a sign and commandment given by the *Shariya* for Muslims. We have it in common, though there are differences in the timing and form of the rite. Muslim and Jew are both connected to God in this way.

MY SON, MY SON

As a father of sons, I too have experienced the anguish of such decision-making. When my youngest son was born, I recorded my inner experiences with the thought that they might be helpful to others:

My son is almost a week old. I sit at my typewriter, improvising thoughts about the *Bris*. As usual, my thoughts arrange themselves along the four dimensions of doing, feeling, knowing, and being. It is a habit of mind.

Doing: Begin with history, going back to Egypt, where circumcision was practiced. Why did Abraham circumcise in the oak groves of Mem-Re? Because it was Mem-Re who gave him advice concerning circumcision. Circumcision had made sense in ancient Egyptian spirituality; it was one of the ways high consciousness and great knowledge were transmitted. Who knows to what extent *Milah* influences culture?

Perhaps something destructive and "macho" gets refined by a *Bris*, directing a man away from pure instinct and toward prudent judgment. I scanned my life and saw how many times I had made decisions contrary to the urgings of my instincts, difficult decisions which turned out for the best and were right. Was this because of *Milah*?

Maybe Freud was right about the dominating power of the libido: if so, it makes sense to take that absolute power away from the penis. I want my child to have this advantage over instinct.

So much of what happens in sex is covenantal. Perhaps this is why Covenant has to be imposed on this organ from the very first.

Then I think of the *mohel* (ritual circumciser). Much depends on him: who he is; what he does; what tools he uses; how self-conscious or assured he is. His emotional state is important. What feelings or tensions will he telegraph to the baby? Will he love the baby at least a little bit, and hold him firmly and warmly enough to make him feel safe?

I imagine the *mohel* and a thought begins to take shape in the back of my mind. If the world will be cruel to my son, and sooner or later we will all feel pain, let me mercifully and gently introduce him to it myself, rather than leave it to someone who did not love him before and will not love him after. The thought occurs to me to be the *mohel* for my son.

I look into the future and want to see a world in which there are Jews. The world is richer because of us, more civilized. I want my children and grandchildren to live in a world in which Jewish questions are being asked, like the one that exercises me at this moment and makes me consult my world of ethics and morals to make a life decision.

Abraham was not satisfied to perform circumcision on the advice of Mem-Re alone. He wanted God to command him. Oy! How strongly I relate to his desire at this moment. I feel and know that I cannot do this to my child for idealism alone. I cannot take the whole responsibility on myself. All my good notions are not enough. There is a moment of risk: what if the knife slips? All the catastrophic possibilities arise as risks I fear to take alone. I can't do it by myself. I need God's command. By way of answer, an image rushes through my mind in which I see my penis, from which my son came, and my father's penis, from which I came, and all the penises of all the fathers back to Abraham and the moment he received

God's command: ". . . every male among you shall be circumcised; the foreskin of his penis shall be cut off. This will be the proof that you and they accept this covenant."

Feeling: "Lonely" and "connected" are the words that come to mind. Foreskin (*Orlah*), a stopped-up dullness, is removed, leaving a penis sharply exposed, vulnerable yet intimate when caressed, standing erect, full of consciousness. We have been taught to cover our private parts, but privately we know we have a *Bris* which connects us with others. Marked forever as a Jew.

Taking a child to the *Bris* is a sacrifice. It is a death that is not fatal. It is the first time my child will get close to being a sacrifice, his first at-one-ment and holymaking. All the other nonfatal deaths that will occur are contained and made safe in this one.

Why do this to a child who has no control, instead of waiting for him to do it himself? The Jew says, "Because it is better so, and I as parent take responsibility." There is an aspect of being Jewish that goes beyond a mere private matter between a soul and her God. My father *wanted* me to be Jewish, and my children and my children's children, all the way to the end of time. And so do I.

Of all the tests of my loyalty, this test of the *Bris Milah* is the hardest. Yet there can be only one outcome. All my cells know it. I feel my refusal to participate would deny my son the option of a vital Jewish life.

Then I look at my son and my resolve weakens. In the here and now, there are not enough reasons to do the Bris. My baby is, flesh of my flesh and blood of my blood, while the history resides only in my feelings—the same feelings that program me to protect my child.

What would I do if a deranged cultist were to sneak in and circumcise my son for the sake of his private madness? I would destroy him. I am not an absolute pacifist when it comes to protecting my children. And yet it is I, Zalman as mohel, who am about to do this unspeakable thing to my child.

Knowing: In my world of thoughts, the pros and cons endlessly cancel each other out. Inclinations toward culture and against brute instinct are cancelled out by a natural sense that the baby is already perfect as he is. Thoughts in support of the Mishpoche and the clan are cancelled out by the messianic vision that we are all one clan and there is no need for such divisions for the good of humankind.

But bigger thoughts roll to the center of my awareness, thoughts of the limits of my understanding and the finiteness of my mind. Be humble vis-a-vis God and your ancestors, these thoughts say, the tradition is ancient and collective, and you are only one. One Jewish man among all Jewish men. And so too is your son.

My thoughts move full circle. The Bris Milah of my son is inevitable. And I myself shall perform it. Myself. My son.

Being: As God exists in relationship to humans in his AM-NESS ("I AM THAT I AM"), so in some smaller way do I stand in relationship to my son. In the am-ness of my being as father, I sired him

with sperm from my body, and shall protect,
provide for, and prepare him until he becomes
himself, on his own, to be whatever it is he will be.
As my own *Bris*, among many other experiences,
helped to shape my being, so shall his.

I cannot end these observations about the *Bris* of our
sons without addressing a very great question—what
about our daughters? What ceremonial act initiates them
into the Jewish Covenant with God? The fact is that there
is no Jewish female equivalent to a *Bris* (nor would any
reasonable person suggest that a rite of excision be instituted). The roots of this situation lie in the patriarchal
past, where our heritage begins. Tradition, of course, car-
ries great importance in the unfolding of our lives, but we
must also be concerned with the present. Judaism is
evolving, is attempting to meet the needs of real people
here and now. The reality is that we must discover or
allow for the revelation of a ritual for girls that will serve
the covenantal function performed for boys by the *Bris*.

THE DANCE OF
SABBATH

It is Friday night and my thoughts are turned toward Sabbath. A wave of forgiveness flows through me and I feel a sense of well-being for all the creatures in the universe. This is an expansive feeling, part of the sense of God's plenty that arrives with the coming of Sabbath.

On the eve of Sabbath, the Jewish home is filled with the aromas of God's cornucopia, telling of an abundance that is greater than all our needs, real or imagined. This sense of God's abundance is luxurious. Despite the urgency of preparing for Sabbath, it relaxes me. I feel loved and cared for, and my usual workday worries begin to fall away. Even the deepest knots loosen up.

Friday afternoon is a mixture of opposites, a give-and-take between the tension of preparing for Sabbath and the deep relaxation of being in it. The preparations are like a dance; we develop a rhythm and work up a fine sweat, but it is the sweat of pleasure, not of hard work.

Like most dances, the preparing-for-Sabbath dance is best done with other people. The household hums with satisfaction as all the members go about their tasks of getting ready. We bump into each other as the pace

quickens, but we do not mind. We smile at each other in
our shared concern—we are comrades, partners; we are
lovers.

During the six days of the week, we are bidden to *do*.
On the Sabbath, we are bidden to cease doing, to refrain
from action. How then can we *live* on the Sabbath?

You may say: "I want to make the Sabbath a rest. My
problem is *how*."

What you need is a functional recipe for Sabbath action
and nonaction. Verbal descriptions or prescriptions are
not enough. To learn to drive a car you need more than
verbal instruction, nor are you equipped to drive even if
you understand the principles of the internal combustion
engine. You must be taught, not in a conceptual or verbal
way, but nonverbally. In the same way, you can learn to
acquire what I call the nonverbal body language that goes
into observing the Sabbath.

In earlier times, the worst epithet you could give to
another Jew was *am ha'aretz*: 'unlettered peasant.' An *am
ha'aretz* was a man who did not even know the translation
of a simple blessing over food, although he recited it
faithfully in Hebrew on every occasion. Yet, in comparison with his modern counterpart, such a man was a Jewish sophisticate. Our ignoramus was at least able to *do* the
right thing. He knew when to genuflect; he knew all the
synagogue responses by heart and reeled them off automatically at the proper cue. And as far as the Sabbath was
concerned, he had a full repertoire of proper body responses. He may not have been able to tell you much
about the theological and social ideas embodied in the
Sabbath, but *he knew what to do and how to live on the
Sabbath*.

The opening lines of one of our Sabbath table hymns would not give you any taste or smell association. But it would have aroused such associations in the *am ha'aretz* of former times. Even a bagels-and-lox Jew in our time could not hold a candle to our ignoramus, who would be a connoisseur in comparison. Our ignoramus knew by nonverbal stimuli when to be joyous and when to be sad. To him, the melodies of the liturgy were distinct cues, and his feelings and responses were profoundly Jewish, whereas ours are materialistic or, at best, western or Protestant.

Were I to say to a group of Jews, "Let us pray," the likelihood is that many would bow their heads in Protestant fashion. Few would adjust their hats, feel for the prayer sash, reach out for the little laver at the synagogue entrance to wash their hands, or get ready to assume the proper Jewish prayer stance. Our minds may be Jewish, but our bodies are Protestant. It is for these reasons that we find it difficult to learn how to live the Sabbath properly.

We must acquire a new language, or actually reacquire a forgotten one. This language is emotive and rich in the imagery of feelings. It resides in our bodies and is not conceptual or logical.

This language is not for our reason, but for our imagination; not for the intellect, but for our muscular responses. It is a language in which we must expect anthropomorphisms. In this tongue, God can be a man—fatherly, kingly—and the Sabbath a bride—a woman, a queen, and very much the ideal mother.

We do not concretize our projections by making them into material objects like statues. Nevertheless, God as King, and the Sabbath as Queen are real symbols, living and life-giving symbols possessing limitless energy. By using these symbols, we do not imply that our reason is inadequate. People's reason is not weak; it is very strong. It is the greatest gift God has given us. But reason cannot teach the language we now have to acquire to be able to enter into the Sabbath. For, like the man in Kafka's tale, *Before the Law*, we may be condemned to spend our entire lives at the gate, our very own gate, and never enter into the Law unless we acquire this language which I call body Hebrew or body Yiddish.

In this language, weekdays are masculine, or at least we are masculine in our response to weekdays; even women tend to be masculine in their weekday response.

During the week, we *husband* the earth, we *husband* our strength. Then comes the Sabbath and we become feminine. We receive, we conceive, we are impregnated with a supernal soul, and we give birth to a tenderness. In looking at the Sabbath in feminine terms, we do not mean sex or imply Freudian libido. We mean a tendency to a rich empathic quality. For on the Sabbath, we regenerate a warmth expressed by the term *rachamim* (*rachmones* in Yiddish). *Rachamim* is usually translated as *pity*, a cold word, or as *mercy*, an antiseptic one, or sometimes as *compassion*. In the final analysis, *rachamim*, derived from *rechem*, meaning womb, is not quite translatable into English. Our task, however, is not to translate these feelings into another verbal language, but to translate them into the deep language of our bodies and our very beings.

We do not live deliberately enough. We use the verb, *to live*, in a faulty manner. When I say "I live," I, the subject, use the word *live* in its active form. And yet there is so much of my living that is determined: I am *being lived* by heredity, by environment, by society, by rules. Only when I make a deliberate effort, and switch off a number of habitual and automatic acts before they dictate my behavior, can I say that I live or that I love, or that I "sabbath." For it is the duty and the privilege of the Jew to be able to "make the Sabbath."

That is what we must learn: to "sabbath" a Sabbath. It is not altogether impossible because we are not called upon to do something we have never done before. We often live in a Sabbath mode during our regular day, though we may not have labeled it that.

There are two nervous systems in humans, the sympathetic and the parasympathetic. The sympathetic nervous system concerns itself with aggression and defense; it speeds up the heartbeat; it prepares the body for flight or fight. A person is far more determined and far less deliberate when he finds himself in the sympathetic mode of being. If we had to live only that mode, we would burn ourselves out within a short time.

The action of the parasympathetic system is quite different. In this mode we digest, eat, sleep, and procreate. The physical system operates at a far slower pace; the heart beats more slowly; we breathe more deeply; and all energies flow down the center. We could compare the sympathetic mode of being to the weekday mode, and the parasympathetic mode to the Sabbath one.

On the Sabbath, we must learn to awaken parasympathetically. All spiritual authors agree that the parasympathetic mode of being plays a great part in high spiritual achievement. Hence we must condition and reinforce this mode. We must feel *shabbasdig* (sabbathly), see, smell, and hear *shabbasdig*, and have a total *shabbasdig* consciousness. How can we do this?

Let me suggest a process. Try to validate it in the laboratory of your Sabbath experience. If it works, you can do it again. If not, you may discard it, for it may not suit your own personal body rhythm or situation, and to keep it up as part of your Sabbath repertoire may hinder you instead of help.

1. *Hurried exertion.* This is a preparation. The mind must be filled with urgency. Soon it will be Sabbath! You do not eat a full meal at noon, in order to work up hunger and not merely an appetite. You work up a sweat. According to some of our spiritual authors, that is considered more purifying than a number of fast days because, by this muscular exertion, the entire body enters into the service of God.

2. Clean the house, even if it is already clean, or very little is left to put in order. Bathe in honor of the Sabbath, shave or fix your hair. If you can, take a dip in a lake or pool.

3. Now ease the pace deliberately. Hum a melody slowly. Change your clothes, choose some items that you never wear except on the Sabbath. Put some money aside for *tzedakah* (charity) to be deposited in a *tzedakah* box before kindling the Sabbath lights.

4. Sit somewhere where you can be alone, not talking. Do *teshuvah* (repentance) for the week. Let the week's events pass before your mind's eye. Sift the good from the bad, hold the bad up to God and ask to be forgiven. If there is anyone whom you angered during the week, seek him out; ask his forgiveness, become reconciled to God and man. Breathe deeply, recollect some more, and center down to the parasympathetic mode of consciousness. Be careful to shift your senses to the Sabbath mood. Practice what Abraham Joshua Heschel calls "radical amazement"—see everyday things for the miracles they are.

5. Light the candles, study a little Torah. If a particular historic personage intrigues you especially, invite him or her for the Sabbath to be your guest in spirit.

6. Accept upon yourself the rule of no weekday talk, no trivialities, no "lines." If possible, shift to Hebrew. Franz Rosenzweig found the practice of no weekday talk especially helpful on the Sabbath.

7. Come early for the service and, before it begins, pray for the ability to serve God in the service.

8. Serve—participate—respond—read *out*, not *in*. Address Him. During moments of quiet, be passive and don't force any particular meditation on the Sabbath. This forcing is for the week. Allow the liturgy to speak for you; give it assent by investing energies into chanting, into reading, into silence.

9. Intend to enter into the celebrant's *kiddush* (sanctification of the Sabbath time over wine), thus giving testimony to God's blessed creatorship. Drink the wine as a special gift from the hand of Mother Sabbath. Before you seat yourself at the table, wash your hands and eat some of the *challah*-loaf after the blessing. Relish the eating as a *mitzvah*, a holy act, dipping the bread in salt first. Eat with little talking except of things pertaining to the Sabbath, to Torah and to prayer. Sing slowly and benignly. During the meal, intend to be like a priest who offers the mineral, animal, and vegetable kingdoms to God. Imagine that you are the offering and the table is the altar. Enjoy the food by chewing it slowly, and give thanks for the sense-pleasure with which God has endowed the body.

10. Chant some of the table hymns out of the prayer book. Then recite the grace after meals slowly and gratefully. Be present in every word you say. Then take a little silent walk with a friend.

11. When the whole evening is over, say your going-to-bed prayers. Once you pronounce the words, "Into Thy hand," do not speak again until you wake up in the morning. In your thoughts, give thanks to God for the Sabbath up to now. Settle down into a relaxed sleep, all the while being aware that you are being held up by the "everlasting Arms."

Each of these points could have been illustrated by many insightful stories from the Hasidic tradition. I am leaving them out on purpose. The stories will come; you yourselves will live them with God's help.

The Lentchner Rebbe said, "I like the mitzvah of the Succah best, for it is such a holy mitzvah one can enter it even with one's boots!" When the Rebbe, the Yehudi, heard this, he remarked, "I like the mitzvah of Sabbath best, for out of the Succah you can walk at any time, but no one can walk out of the Sabbath."

A TIME FOR
LOVERS

braham Joshua Heschel used to say, "We Jews live more in time than we do in space." "The Sabbath," he would say, "is a palace in Time."

As courtiers dwelling in the palace, we have a special affinity for the texture of time. From the Sabbath perspective we can understand things about time that weekday-driven beings are oblivious to. We call our Holy Days by the name Yom Tov—a good day. Passover is a good time and the Ninth of Av—commemorating the destruction of the Temple in space—a bad time. We know of pressured Sabbath eve time, and of relaxed summer Sabbath afternoon times. We experience time more solemnly on the eve of Yom Kippur than on the eve of Purim. We know the radical difference between what is important and what is pressing, but we often yield the important under the duress of what is pressing.

Where time becomes pressing, it says, "You better get it together, that's a deadline, a deadline." The dread that people have about the experience of a deadline is very strong. It is as if someone says, "Up to here, you're alive, but when you hit that line, you're dead."

The Sabbath is an antidote to dead time. It is the day for going to the inner garden of our imaginations to meet with God. The garden is lush and peaceful, hung with memories and consolations, trailing tenderness and dreams. There are pools in which we see ourselves being fully understood and accepted; our thoughts of appreciation bloom.

The Sabbath is for lovemaking. Making love is the ideal model of the relationship between God and His/Her people. In the right conditions, it is a holy act. When our intentions are to give love as well as receive it, and when we consciously interact with our partner in a dance of mutual caring, lovemaking is a *mitzvah*, a good deed.

In the act of making love, we connect with each other and with God. It is a deep connection, strong yet subtle, sometimes elusive. We have to warm to each other, get into the same rhythm. So it is important to take time for the prelude, to embrace and kiss.

The Baal Shem Tov taught, "It was revealed to me from above that the reason for the delay in the coming of the Messiah is that people do not enter the mystery of the kiss before the great loving."

GODBIRTHING

Many people who are "born again" don't know that there is more than one brand of that experience available. Being born again is getting plugged into the universe, and no single religion has a monopoly on the universe. David sings in the Psalms as having heard the Voice proclaim: "You are my child. Today I have begotten you."

Imagine a person who has a terrible life. Everything always goes wrong and he doesn't know where to turn or what to do. And in the midst of this he has the insight— the revelation, if you will—that the universe is not an accident, that everything going on in his life is part of the payment for wiping him clean. For a Christian, this revelation happens at the moment he takes Jesus into his life and Jesus tells him, "I am doing it for you." Jesus brings him atonement and floods him with warmth. "You are forgiven," Jesus tells him, and the picture is so big, the universe so vast, that the little problems of life are nothing compared to the flash of love and acceptance at this instant.

There are many paths to that experience. Jesus is one way of getting it, and fasting is another way of getting it, and making love or meditating are others. It can happen anywhere. You can get it in the middle of jogging, or in a split second while you are stuck in traffic. And you can get it during orgasm, when you're forgiven and loved. Whenever you get it, it's Yom Kippur.

Being born again occurs in time, but I'm not talking about time as it exists in its quantifiable, measurable aspects—the parceled-out time of the calendar. On that level, Yom Kippur can only be on the tenth day of Tishrey, which falls each year on such-and-such a day in September or October. Rather, I mean the Yom Kippur which exists all the time.

We Jews make a strong, concerted movement in the direction of the eternal atonement by recycling the Yom Kippur experience once a year. And we always do it in recognition of the historical moment when our people had the first total born-again experience—the exodus from Egypt. That was when we "heard" God say in the desert, "You are forgiven."

This voice comes to us from the totality of our tradition, but also from deep within ourselves.

"You are my child, today I have begotten you," the Psalm says. When a person "hears" this, birthing has begun. But to stop the process at this point would leave the soul in infancy. Being born again is not enough; you have to grow up, too. All growth happens in stages. First, you grow through the stage of "the land of milk and honey," when the world sings and supports the newly born God-spark in you. The feeling is intoxicating. Some people are so addicted to this phase that they move from one spiritual path and leader to another, hoping to avoid the next phase, when the path becomes discipline. Like a child in toilet training, they rebel against the external authority and boundary-setting which the discipline phase requires. Thank God, this phase does not last forever.

In the next phase, you are filled with excitement and

enthusiasm as you tune in to all the symbols of the tradition. Each one resonates with meaning for you. In this
phase, you like to communicate and interact mostly with
those who share your symbol system. This love for the
people with whom you share grows vast and powerful and
urges you to work toward the establishment of a holy
community. And there is more growth ahead as you move
toward the maturity of the soul, the phase in which you
live in intimate closeness with the Beloved.

Godbirths vary. The classic born-again experience is a
sudden, discontinuous event. For the person growing
with God in daily practice, there is likely to be less drama.
The experience will be more gentle, natural, and easier on
your immediate family.

Higher spirals of spiritual growth are not for a book;
they call for a spiritual apprenticeship. If you stay with
this work, you have every reason to trust the adage,
"When the pupil is ready, the teacher appears."

I BELIEVE WE
CAN RISE UP

I Believe.

It has been the struggle of my life to overcome my doubts, my limited comprehension, my ignorance. In my youth I was filled with bitterness at what was happening to me and all the other Jews of Europe. My first experiences with Hasidic mysticism opened the door to the living God, and my bitterness began to drain away, to diminish. I understood and felt it in a different way. But I would not be honest if I did not reveal the mighty awe I feel whenever I think of the six million Jews and the millions of non-Jews who perished in the Holocaust. It was the death of a world.

It has not been my intention to attempt an apology, to try to explain God's ways to man. What I have tried to do is transmit some of the spiritual legacy of that world as it applies to our own.

As these last pages are being written, the radio has announced the death of the Dutchman Victor Kugler at the age of eighty-one. Kugler was the man who hid Anne

Frank and her family from the Nazis. In the time of Satan, it was an act of God. In the midst of destruction and madness came an act of courage and love. But in the end, the Franks were discovered, and shared the fate of European Jewry.

After the Holocaust, many survivors lost their faith: if God exists, how could this have happened!

Others didn't deny God's existence; they became filled with anger instead. Some persist in raging against a God who let it occur. I cannot argue with this rage. But I will repeat the words spoken by Rebbe Barukh of Medzebozh to one of his disciples: "I know there are questions that have no answers; there is a suffering that has no name; there is injustice in God's creation—and there are reasons enough for man to explode with rage. I know there are reasons for you to be angry. Good. Let us be angry. Together."*

The questions remain. What do we believe? Do we believe at all? And how do our beliefs bring us together and help us live in greater harmony and do a better job with our lives?

For those of you who do not believe, I have no answers. As part of my believing, I pray for you. And I ask that you do one thing in return. Now. As you read these words.

Sit where you are. Sit there *as if.* As if you believe that God exists, that He or She is as real as a rock, a tree, a bird, your hand, your heart; as if She is as real as the inner you, where your most secret feelings are, your pain and fear and wonder and hope and longing and love and strength and weakness.

*As translated by Elie Wiesel in *Four Hasidic Masters* (University of Notre Dame Press, Notre Dame, 1978). I understand "together" to include everyone, Jews and non-Jews alike.

Sit there as if you and God are both naked, hiding nothing of your need, your want. And say it: "I want. I need. I don't deserve. All I can do is say I am here. I am open to the universe, of which I am a natural part. I accept the universe. I ask the universe to accept me. Please."

Have you ever made a private vow, a secret promise in a tense moment of stress or fear?

If only I get out of this, I will . . .

If she survives the operation, I will . . .

If only the baby is born healthy, I will . . .

The thing you promise to do is important, it is a sacrifice. But the Being or Presence in front of whom you make your promise, your vow, is more important. It is your God.

When you make this kind of inner vow, you are turning to God as He exists within you. It is a deeply instinctive and visceral move, an action whose roots extend so far into your past that it is beyond your capacity for rational comprehension. This inner vow is based on the preverbal, precognitive knowledge we carry in the marrow of our bones; it is encoded in the DNA in every cell in our bodies.

The vow can also be seen as magical because it is based on the assumption (often unarticulated) that our thoughts and feelings can have an effect on the workings of the world. Reb Nachman stated the case directly: "Know that there are great powers in man. By thought alone one can achieve a great deal."

This process, which fuses and aims the energies of our thoughts, feelings, and our very physical beings, is prayer in one of its highest forms. It can be said that the object of prayer is the well-being of the universe.

Prayer is the energy feedback God gets from us, His creation. Prayer completes the circuit of God's energy and helps to keep it flowing. Praying for ourselves or our loved ones contributes energy to the entire system, for we are integral parts of the universe. Praying for our well-being, and ultimately for our own perfection, is equal to praying for the universe, since it is composed of its parts, of us.

We all know that prayer can be difficult. Many of us have been put off, dissociated from our natural place in the order of things, disconnected from our own sense that we belong and that we matter.

Prayer unifies, it unites us with our fellow human beings and all the other beings in God's universe. Taken in our totality—gentile and Jew; woman and man; child and adult; animal and plant; the earth below and the heavens above—we are the likeness of God.

Our task is clear. We are here to fulfill our potential for Godliness. Even with all our weaknesses and faults, we strive toward that great and sustaining goal. And if perfection seems remote, beyond the possibilities of our limitations, all we have to do is work toward improvement.

We work to follow God's will, which we understand to be the natural laws of the universe as they are encoded in our tradition.

We place ourselves before God and open ourselves to Him—fully disclose our tears and laughter; weaknesses and strengths, certainties and doubts; the parts of ourselves we love and the parts we despise; our prides and shames.

In doing this, we open ourselves to the world, to our

fellow humans. We take down the barriers, drop our masks, and join with the rest of creation in the unending effort to live the good life and attain perfection.

Even if we can manage only one step at a time, this journey must be made. In the end, it is the only journey worth making.

When we hold hands with all creation and sing praises to God, the Lord of the Cosmos, we are fulfilling our role in the universe.

Judaism, like life itself, is organic. Neither is perfect; both are evolving. Each generation learns what it can. Every incarnation brings a soul to more light.

We are all on our way to the messianic finale, when the total consciousness of all the inhabitants of this planet is moved to one great at-one-ment.

We look forward to this event with the hope that it will be peaceful and organic. But the shadow of planetary self-destruction hovers over us. There is a real fear that the finale will be fire and destruction, that the earth's apotheosis will start with a nuclear flash and end with a dead planet circling through space.

For our part, we must strive to prevent destruction and bring about salvation, for ourselves and our planet. The finale can also be a quantum leap in our awareness of how the universe works, the beginning of a new and higher way of life rather than the fiery end of an old one.

One of the strongest teachings I've yet received on reincarnation came from the present Lubavitcher Rebbe, Rabbi Menachem Mendel Schneerson Shlit"a, who once said, "The teachings on gilgul—reincarnation—are true, AND, it is also true that you don't have to wait to die to start a new life. In turning to God (teshuvah), you can start the next reincarnation right now."

That being or sum of beings that we call Messiah is held prisoner in the surface tensions existing between person and person, men and women, older and younger, richer and poorer, group and group, nation and nation. Wherever tensions and resistances are reduced, so that energy can be shared, the quantum leap is made to the Messianic era.

The Messianic future, with its blessings, awaits us at the other side of our awakening, so let us light the candles of our souls and welcome the Sabbath.

ABOUT THE AUTHORS

RABBI ZALMAN SCHACHTER-SHALOMI has been at the forefront of a pioneering renewal of Jewish spirituality in the contemporary world. Through prayer and meditation, movement and song, story-telling and philosophical discourse, he presents the central teachings of Hasidism and Kabbalah in a contemporary manner which makes them accessible to everyone. Reb Zalman awakens and inspires the process which connects the individual to the living God. He has touched the lives of many people who have discovered spiritual fulfillment through Judaism and Torah.

Born in Poland in 1924, and raised in Vienna, Austria, he was imprisoned as a youngster by the Vichy-French government. In 1941 he came to the United States and entered the Lubavitch Yeshiva, where he was ordained in 1947. Reb Zalman received a Master of Arts in the Psychology of Religion from Boston University, and a Doctor of Letters from Hebrew Union College.

He has been a congregational rabbi, a Hebrew school principal, a Hillel Foundation director, and a resource consultant and spiritual guide for individuals and for Jewish communities throughout North America and Israel. For twenty years he was a Professor of Religion and Head of the Department of Near Eastern and Judaic Studies at the University of Manitoba, Canada. Since 1975 he has been Professor of Religion in Jewish Mysticism and Psychology of Religion at Temple University in Philadelphia.

Reb Zalman has published over 150 articles and monographs on the Jewish spiritual life, and has translated many Hasidic and Kabbalistic texts. He is author of *Fragments of a Future Scroll: Hasidism for the Aquarian Age*. He is also known to many as the *Zayde* of the *Jewish Catalog*.

His interest in the universality of spiritual truths has led Reb Zalman to study with Sufi masters, Buddhist teachers, Native American Elders, Catholic monks, and humanistic and transpersonal psychologists. His synthesis of these wide-ranging experiences makes his teaching unique and invaluable.

Reb Zalman lives in Philadelphia with his wife Elana and their two children, Shalvi and Barya. As Rebbe of B'nai Or Religious Fellowship, he provides the spiritual guidance and vision to an organization dedicated to Jewish spiritual renewal in the contemporary world.

DONALD GROPMAN was born and raised in Boston, Massachusetts. He is a graduate of Brandeis University and received a Masters Degree from the Writers' Workshop of San Francisco State College. He has published numerous articles and reviews. His short stories have appeared in several anthologies, including *The Best American Short Stories*. He is the author of *Say It Ain't So, Joe!* for which he was named a Knight of Mark Twain by the Mark Twain Journal for his contribution to American biography.

He lives in western Massachusetts with his wife, the sculptor Gabrielle Rossmer, and their two children, Sonya and Adam.

HOW THIS BOOK WAS WRITTEN

When we came together to write this book, we set the tasks this way: Zalman would provide the material, Don would give it form and a voice. For the most part we followed our own guidelines, but collaborations such as this are never clear-cut. Hence, some of the writing is Zalman's; some of the ideas are Don's.

The nature of our process was exchange—Zalman identified content, Don gave it shape. Our work took us to classes in Jewish mysticism, a conference on The Higher Spirituality, a Fabrangen at the Lubavitch Center in Brooklyn, weekend prayer retreats, synagogue services and Havurah gatherings. We met for work sessions at B'nai Or in Philadelphia, in Boston, New York, western Massachusetts, Connecticut and at Bennington College in Vermont. But wherever we worked, the essential process was the same—one long conversation in which we explored and tried to distill a whole world of ideas, emotions and experiences. We came together as colleagues, we parted as friends.

—DG AND ZS-S